P.T.S

A SELF-HELP SURVIVAL GUIDE

NOT FOR CIVVIES, DO-GOODERS, AND THOSE EASILY OFFENDED!

Copyright & Disclaimer

This book is dedicated to all the brave men and women of every country, who were, are, or will be prepared to endure desperate hardships, suffer life altering injuries, or make the ultimate sacrifice; so civilians can be spared the horrors and ravages of war.

I also dedicate it to the memory of a good shipmate; AB(R) Mark "Snowy" Winter.

Forward

Here's a piece of personal history guaranteed to put you to sleep; I have never served in the Armed Forces and I am a card carrying member of Civvy Street. However that being said, I was formally diagnosed with C-PTSD. I won't go into all the boring details, suffice to say I experienced chronic abuse throughout my childhood and early teens. I learned the art of dissociation early; hence I was often called the Ice Queen.

I worked in and around the Justice arena for upwards of 20 years. In this time I witnessed human kind at its worst. My work involved victims, offenders and entire communities in crisis. Imagine walking into a community as a single female - one where male co-workers refused to go - witnessing domestic brutality, sexual brutality (yes incest), addictions and murder. Imagine a child of 12 years burning down their day care because it represented to them a place not even belonging in our worst nightmares, and you will begin to understand the kind of environment I worked in.

My schooling was centred on criminology and justice. I trained in delivering Community Justice Forums - similar to mediation - and worked in community development.

Since my diagnosis I have become a voracious researcher on PTSD. I spent nearly forty years thinking I was broken or defective as a human being. The road I travelled was one of alcohol and drugs, just to take the edge off. I even came close to succeeding in meeting our maker on several occasions. I tried prescription medication (this was over 20 years ago) but they made me feel like a zombie. Get that thought gone; I'm not talking about the Hollywood flesh eating kind! Mind you, my kids have accused me of chewing their heads off numerous times.

Stuart and I briefly chatted about hypnosis and he sent me a link to an article he had written entitled "EFT for PTSD"; and I was intrigued. It took me a while to finish the initial article, because whilst reading, I had actually started crying and wished someone like him had been around all those years ago. PTSD is easily misunderstood to those who cannot comprehend life's horrors.

Stuart has accomplished a feat which no other could; he has written a book geared for the most macho of military men, right down to us civvies. In this book you will find clear, concise and easy to read information not only on PTSD, but also on various treatments. He has given enough information on each, so you the reader can make an informed decision before you broach the subject with your doctor as to which would be best for your individual circumstance.

The use of humour keeps the reader from being overwhelmed by negative thoughts and feelings. I must admit I haven't been able to look at my shrubs the same since reading this book, and I laugh at my own internal imagery whenever I look out my windows now.

Stuart reminds you that you are neither 'broken nor damaged', because you have either experienced, witnessed, or both, some traumatic experience. He reassures you, life does get easier and you can manage and lessen the symptoms of your PTSD.

The advice given is sound: from finding someone to talk to, which does help ease the burden of that which you carry inside; to writing stories, poetry, or music to just get your feelings out there into the light of day; to using your senses to see, smell, taste, listen and touch as a reminder to yourself that there is beauty in the world, even during our darkest moments.

If you choose to take nothing else from this book for which ever reason you come up with; at the very least try out the 10 bonus tips, they are more than worth it. Don't let the words 'New Age' put you off; as Stuart says, these come from ancient times. You may even be unconsciously practicing some of them yourself.

Read this book, and then reread the parts you want to give a try. Give it to your spouse and family to read, as it will also help them in understanding what you are experiencing.

You have been provided with enough information to try Hypnosis and EFT safely within your home. So now you can practice your chosen technique in privacy, if you aren't comfortable with the thought of having someone around. However as Stuart states; always consult your doctor before changing your treatment plan. Don't be afraid to try something new.

Now here's my tangent; read it then reread it, practice and keep practicing the techniques, and then reread it again. Keep a diary; look back on your successes and improvements. Baby steps are the key to success because there is no magic wand or instant cure.

Yes and congratulations on taking the first step; opening this book with the intention of reading it. Now give yourself a pat on the back and carry on!

Sincerely,

Maureen Scott

Native of Manitoba, Canada, & Currently Residing in Scotland.

Contents

Section 1: Information About PTSD

Section 2: Treatments For PTSD

Section 3: EFT For PTSD

Section 4: Bonus Tips

2nd Disclaimer

The content of this book is for information only.

You are solely responsible for the way in which you use this information.

The personal opinions expressed in this booklet are just that and nothing more; which is the right of the author in accordance with the Universal Declaration of Human Rights, Article 19 which states:

"Everyone has the right to freedom of opinion and expression; this right includes freedom to hold opinions without interference and to seek, receive and impart information and ideas through any media and regardless of frontiers."

(Everyone else seems to hide behind Human Rights, so thought I may as well give it a go!)

The techniques you are about to read are "Complimentary" Therapy and not "Alternative" therefore:

- Always consult with a Doctor when you believe you are suffering from any condition that may be impairing your mental (or physical) abilities.
- Never cease taking prescribed medication without first obtaining permission from a Doctor or other qualified person.

PTSD is a serious and underestimated problem for Service Personnel. Support is out there.

One of the Organisations I personally recommend in the U.K. is the charity "Combat Stress". They are not in any way responsible or associated with the content of this book or its author.

For further information visit: www.combatstress.org.uk

Fun Disclaimers

1.   If I offend anyone reading this book, I'm genuinely sorry you have such low self-esteem; I recommend you go and see a good therapist. Whenever someone has anything of significance to say, they will offend someone. In fact it doesn't even have to be all that significant!

2.   If I inadvertently made a politically incorrect remark without knowing about it, firstly; get a grip on reality. Everyone is different from everyone else, but we all make up one species. Secondly, what is politically correct today may be totally offensive tomorrow. And thirdly, my defence should you want to sue me is the following: "A man in a Victorian suit suddenly appeared in my kitchen, he said his name was Herbert George. He passed me a manuscript for this book and told me to take credit for it, and to not tell anyone, oops; too late, sorry H.G. He then disappeared again in some weird futuristic contraption, honest; you ask Smudge!"

3.   If you start having erotic fantasies about shrubberies after reading this book, it wasn't this book which caused it I assure you. You were probably a Matelot in a previous life!

4. If you are taking offence already; can't you fucking read? The cover of this book clearly says "Not for civvies, do-gooders, or those who are easily offended". Now put the book down and go and complain about the weather or something to someone who is going to give a shit!

5. If some Civvy reads this and thinks I am making light of PTSD, please read this book to the end and then reread it at least 100 times; because you may miss the point and have misunderstood my aims. Oh yes, then go and sign up for the Military, so you can understand what these guys are really going through, not just second guess from what you've seen in the media!

Wouldn't it be great if all "real" disclaimers were like this?!

I hope as you start reading this book, you have a smile on your face; after all it is our great sense of humour which gets us through the tough times when we serve. Now the Legal Crap is out the way, please enjoy and if it helps in anyway; then it was worth my effort.

I recommend getting a pen or pencil to hand before starting this book, so you can highlight any bits of information which you may want to reference later. I do this with all the books I read, so I don't have to spend ages looking through hundreds of pages for a single sentence. If you have any "eureka" moments, you can quickly scribble them down on the page, before they disappear into the ether.

Also, at the end of the bonus tips section, I will ask you to fill in your answer to a question I will pose. So make sure, you at least have a pen or pencil to hand when you start reading the tenth tip.

Introduction

My intention when writing this book was to make it unlike any other on the market; not condescending, overly confusing, and not too pretentious; because I know you are not looking for sympathy, I know you want to be treated like a normal human being, and apart from your symptoms; I know you are just another regular member of the Armed Forces family.

Granted, P.T.S.D. is a very severe and underestimated problem facing ALL Combat Troops, but I didn't want to just create another book which makes you feel far worse, confuses the fuck out of you, or doesn't provide any real solutions.

In some ways I guess I was inspired to write this book in an unconventional style after reading "Radical Honesty" by Brad Blanton. This was the first book I'd read by an eminent psychologist with swearing in it; very refreshing after most of the ones I have read. Another influence may have been the movie "Patch Adams" starring Robin Williams which is based on the life of a real physician, Hunter Doherty Adams MD. If you've never seen it, I highly recommend watching it for some insights on how unconventional thinkers are held back; often to the detriment of those they are trying to help. Although the film is very sad in places, it is also quite hilarious.

This is the reason why I have chosen not to write this like some psychology students stuffy dissertation; there are plenty of them to read if you want to.

I even defied convention by getting an unknown to write the forward to this book. As far as I was concerned, who is there more qualified to review a book on PTSD than someone who suffered the symptoms for forty years? A Doctor or fellow therapist may praise or dismiss certain parts of my writing, they may pick faults or kiss my ass, but they will never be able to empathise with what you are actually going through like Maureen can. Granted, she is a civilian, however if a civvy can make sense of what I have to say, then I know any service person can!

The Psychotherapist part of my persona will deal with the serious aspects of this subject, whilst the Ex-Matelot part will endeavour to inject a little humour.

There will be a few long technical words throughout these pages, but I've kept them to a minimum, and instead tried to speak to you like we were in the mess talking shit, interesting shit though. And of course, I've included a few pretty pictures, because we know we don't like books without them, do we?!

My goal in this work is to, provide you with some answers, allay some doubts, and give you some "food for thought". I'll provide you with some serious facts as I understand them, but I'll also attempt to pepper in a little empathy, humour, and humanity whilst broaching this serious and sensitive subject. Whilst all three of these traits can be found in almost every single serviceman or woman in abundance; it is humour which is going to serve you best in any time of despair. Everyone has heard of the "healing power of laughter", yet few employ it as often as they should.

I want you right now to *remember a time when you were rolling around in fits of hysterics*, who you were with, where you were, and what was so hilarious. If you have served in the Armed Forces, I know you have a ditty or two that make you piss yourself, every time you think about them.

I'm serious, do not read any further until you have a funny memory in your mind.

If you are reading this line, then you must be laughing now, giggling or at the very least tittering. (Tittering; it has the same effect on me as "titmouse" does on Homer Simpson!)

As you recall this great and hysterical time right now, how did you feel during the exact moment?
I'm betting you felt pretty damn good, totally alive and without a worry in the world, yes?

If you're anything like me, I'm sure you're remembering the time vividly right now and thinking *"I'm feeling pretty damn good, totally alive, and I don't have a worry in the world right now!"*

Good, so though I am not a Doctor, I am still going to issue you a prescription: a dose of laughter to be taken as often as possible; at least once a day! The psychological & physiological effects of laughter have been taken so seriously – which is a bit of an oxymoron – there is even a scientific name for its study, "Gelotology"!

So laugh often, laugh loud and laugh hearty my friend.

When we are laughing, happy and feeling good; we are much more forgiving, much more cooperative and even more loving to others. Without going all "hippy" on you, this is the current of the Universe, and when you are in alignment with the Universe, good shit happens! The opposite leaves us feeling alone, bitter and angry with the world. We know the results of this misalignment; all too well.

Branches of Psychology, Physics and Theology all say one thing of a similar nature; your beliefs create your reality. So I want you to believe in yourself, believe you are going to be successful, and most importantly; believe you are going to get better.

Why I've Created This Book Now

Having studied the causes of anxiety and its treatment for a number of years; I am all too aware of the barely recognised situation facing service personnel with regards to PTSD. For all the help which is now emerging to help sufferers of PTSD; there is still not enough. I felt I could contribute, so originally created some videos where I discussed causes, signs and offered some techniques to alleviate the symptoms.

These videos can be found online at this address:

www.youtube.com/user/skilledexforces

In the middle of recording these videos I thought out loud and mentioned possibly creating a short guide to accompany them. This was only supposed to be a quick 10 page PDF at most. Instead I dedicated 2 weeks to creating "Military Transition Tips – EFT for PTSD" which is over 40 pages in length. You should be able to instantly download a copy for FREE at my personal website: www.stuartwelbourn.com

Please don't feel "seen off" for buying this book, because you can receive some of the information for free. If you compare the two, you will easily justify the expense.

Being a bit of a perfectionist, I felt I could still do more to help; so took that first PDF guide, added more content, and turned it into the volume you are now reading.

Because I want you to trust what I have to say is motivated by truly wanting to help, and not by financial gain; I have chosen to donate 100% of my share of profits from sales of this book to the charity "Combat Stress".

There are a lot of organisations and charities now starting to appear, offering support for what is going to be an on-going problem for many years to come. There are also an increasing number of "complementary" therapists setting up in practice; and some of these will be able to help with PTSD. This is good news, PTSD is finally beginning to get the recognition and help it deserves. However the trouble is, the vast majority of sufferers will not qualify for long term help from charities, not come forward for help, or not be able to afford the fees of private consultations. It is for these people I have created this book, the original PDF and accompanying videos.

During my thirteen years working with clients, I successfully helped many to overcome the symptoms of Anxiety and PTSD. Quite a few of these clients were not aware this was the condition they were suffering from, whilst others did not really believe they had a problem at all; a family member had booked the appointment for them.

One reason why people don't seek assistance when they are suffering from PTSD is there is still a slight stigma attached to those seeking help with mental conditions; fortunately this is less than it was a couple of decades ago. For those who have served in the armed forces, and especially for men there is also the fact; it may be perceived as a sign of weakness to admit to not coping after a traumatic experience. Many of the symptoms of PTSD can be embarrassing to talk about; even to a trained professional and so some people just suffer in silence.

Some of the techniques I am going to teach you in this book are often belittled by medical professionals; whilst others say they simply do not work.

Whilst they may not work in every case (nothing does); I assure you they do work with a hell of a lot of people who use them. Although I am quite a sceptical person myself and some of the techniques may seem "new agey" and a bit weird; I have seen almost miraculous results using them.

Some Interesting Statistics

According to the M.O.D. nearly 4000 service men and women from the British Armed Forces were diagnosed with some sort of mental health disorders in 2010. They also reported the most vulnerable age group is 20 -24 year olds, and ratings were twice as likely to suffer as officers, and women twice as likely as men. It may be surprising to learn; only around 63% of cases came from members of the Army. I thought they would make up a higher percentage due to the way they are deployed. Turns out, approximately 25% of the number is made up from the R.A.F, 10% from the Royal Navy and about 2% from the Royal Marines.

In the United States prior to 2002 less than 2000 cases of PTSD were reported on an annual basis. Since involvement in Iraq and Afghanistan this number has increased year after year, reaching a peak of over 16,000 in 2009, before a significant drop in 2010 to less than 10,000.

How It Began & Evolved

Leaving the armed forces and setting up in business is not an easy task. When I began learning more about marketing, I realised many veterans struggle with success when they become self-employed. This was when I decided to take a break from one-to-one consultation and begin a new project to eradicate this problem.

It was whilst working on this new project I came into contact with quite a few "military charities" and discovered providing help sometimes takes second place to making sure there are enough coffers in the bank to pay the wages. I even offered to come down and talk about, and demonstrate (for free) some of the techniques you will soon learn, to PTSD sufferers in the care of one of these organisations; only to be told "oh we wouldn't be interested in anything like that!" To my mind, the most important thing is the end result and not the method, and so this is another reason for putting together this book. Using the techniques outlined in this book and the videos may not rid you of all the symptoms of PTSD, but it could reduce the severity of them.

I created the videos, the original PDF booklet and this book when I could have been using my time to earn money. Unlike many I have encountered in the "healing professions"; helping people is not just a means to an end for me; it is a life purpose.

By making no profit from this work; I have nothing to gain by lying to you. That said; I advise you to not just simply take my word for it, but to do some research for yourself.

As I write this introduction, to prove these techniques work I plan to "put my money where my mouth is". I absolutely hate heights, they scare me shitless. So a few days before this book is planned to be launched I have signed up to do a tandem skydive; and you don't get much higher than this! I'm 100% convinced they will actually get me out of the door on the day, so I will not be doing any work on my fear before then. Later in this book I will hopefully give more details, and share my experience.

My main aim with this work is to help you to help yourself, by providing you with some tools which you can use from the comfort of your own home. Though this book is far from a comprehensive guide to complimentary therapies for P.T.S.D., please do not allow yourself to discard it lightly. I have dedicated many hours to putting this book, the original PDF guide and the videos together for you. When I say dedicated, I mean it quite literally; work/sleep, eat/work/sleep, work/beer/sleep, etc. until it was completed. This pales in significance to the years of study, experience and money I have spent in getting to a point in my life where I can make such a gesture with no other reward than the hope it eases some suffering in the world.

As an Ex-Matelot, I was fortunate when I sailed off to War; I was fairly certain any action we'd be involved in would most likely not be up close and personal. Though I cannot fully empathise with what the "ground troops" are encountering on a daily basis, I do recall; it is the team morale which makes one become "almost" oblivious to the dangers around us. But when we are alone with only our own thoughts and internal chatter for company; this is when the reality of a situation can become truly apparent.

I'm going to be open and frank with you, and let down my defences, so all I ask in return is you to do the same; simply drop any macho pretence, judgment, or preconceived notions for the duration of this book, we can both put back on our "manliness" at the end. Well, you will be able to anyway, mine might take a bit of a kicking in all which is about to be laid bare for the world to see in these pages, and "there ain't no turning back" now!

So read on and let's see if we can't make things just a little better...

Section 1: Information About PTSD

In this section I am going to cover what Post Traumatic Stress Disorder is, what the symptoms are, and a little on the history. We will also briefly look at ordinary stress, anxiety and depression. At the end this section, I have compiled a list of a few do's and do not's of self-treatment, the most important one being; ALWAYS consult with your Doctor first!

Chapter 1

What Is Post-Traumatic Stress Disorder?

To start off with, let's get one thing straight, and out in the open; PTSD is a normal reaction to an abnormal event. Anyone can have an experience which is terrifying, traumatic and out of their control. I'm not talking about waking up next to some crocadilly pig after a particularly heavy run ashore here. I'm actually referring to events such as being involved in a road accident, the victim of an assault or rape, or just simply seeing a traumatic event. Coming under a hail of bullets may be common in a war zone, but is still a frightening experience most would rather not endure. Emergency services staff and Armed Service Personnel are especially prone to encountering traumatic events frequently as part of their vocation; yet they often do not realise they are suffering.

Most people, in time, do get over these unusual and unexpected experiences without needing help. However for some people, these events set off a reaction which can last for months or possibly years. This is what is known as Post-Traumatic Stress Disorder. If you are in a situation where you continue to be exposed to this kind of stress and uncertainty, this will make it extremely difficult, but not impossible for your PTSD symptoms to improve.

Many sufferers do not come forward because of their workload and just allow their symptoms to persist. The sooner you are diagnosed, the sooner you can begin to heal. Suffering in silence, does no one any favours; especially you.

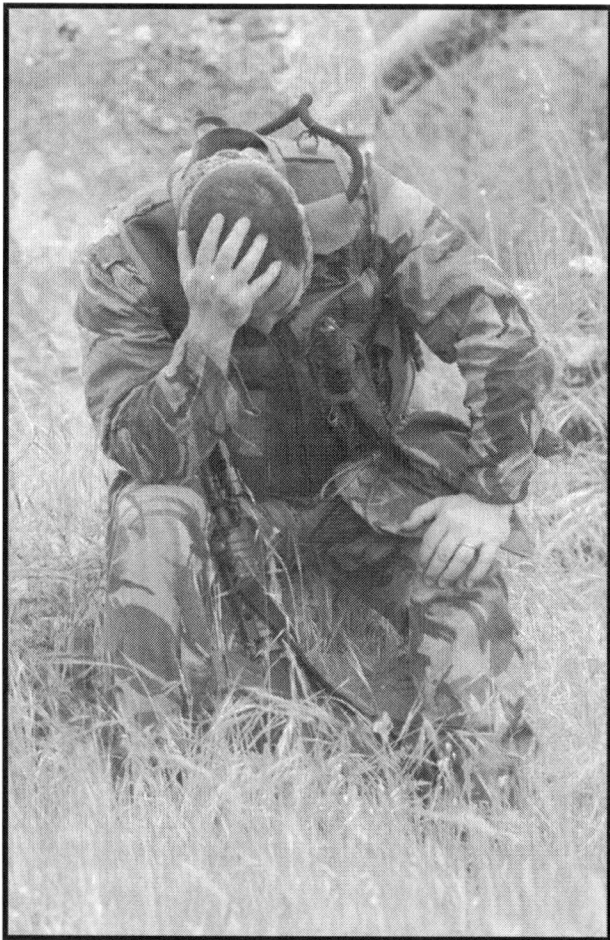

Image 1: There is no need to suffer in silence

Traumatic Events

I once read that about 90% of people will encounter a serious trauma during their lifetimes, but only around 10% of these numbers go on to develop PTSD.

A traumatic event is one in which we believe we are in serious danger, or our life is actually being threatened. Seeing or simply hearing about someone else dying or suffering a severe injury can also cause the onset of PTSD symptoms; especially if it is someone we have a strong emotional bond to. These events challenge our sense of security, of life being fair, and reasonably safe. Such an experience really brings it home; we could die at any time.

The initial symptoms of PTSD are a common and normal reaction to any brush with death kind of experience. Nearly everyone has some symptoms after a trauma. This is natural and it can help to keep you going, help you to understand, and help you to come to terms with the experience. For most people, these symptoms are temporary. They may last for a few days or even weeks, but they progressively lift. Unfortunately, not everyone is so lucky; many find their symptoms persist and really struggle to come to terms with what has happened. If you have post-traumatic stress disorder; the symptoms don't decrease, you don't feel slightly better each day, and you may even start to feel worse. The symptoms of PTSD can start long after the event; a delay of weeks, or even months is much more common than you may think.

You will know you have gotten over the trauma when you can think about it without becoming distressed, not feel constantly threatened, or no longer think about it at inappropriate times.

Chapter 2

What Is The History Of PTSD?

I'll keep the history brief, because although as interesting a subject as it is; it is your future which is of the utmost concern in the creation of this book. The past isn't going to change anything directly, we can only learn from it and hope not to make the same mistakes again; a lesson most politicians seem to ignore!

One of the earliest descriptions of PTSD type symptoms caused by the events of war was made by the Greek historian Herodotus. He described an account of an Athenian soldier who suffered no physical injury from war but became permanently blind after witnessing the death of a fellow soldier during the Battle of Marathon.

The first significant recognition of symptoms - which we now associate with PTSD - on a much wider scale, came during World War I. Known more commonly as "shellshock"; treatment was not very sympathetic because soldiers were not supposed to be afraid during battle. As we know, many people were shot for cowardice during this war. I'm certain it's safe to assume, a great number of these poor Tommie's were suffering from PTSD. The organisation Combat Stress was founded in 1919 & has been helping troops ever since.

In World War II, the story wasn't much better, with one description of the condition being "gross stress reaction", and treatment changing very little since the Great War.

It is only since the end of the Vietnam War, what we now call PTSD began to get wider recognition and useful treatment. There is still a long way to go; but you probably already know this.

Chapter 3

Why Does It Happen?

Whether you are an atheist or religious, the fact remains that human beings have evolved during their history; whether we came from apes, divine intervention or even UFO's dropping us off.

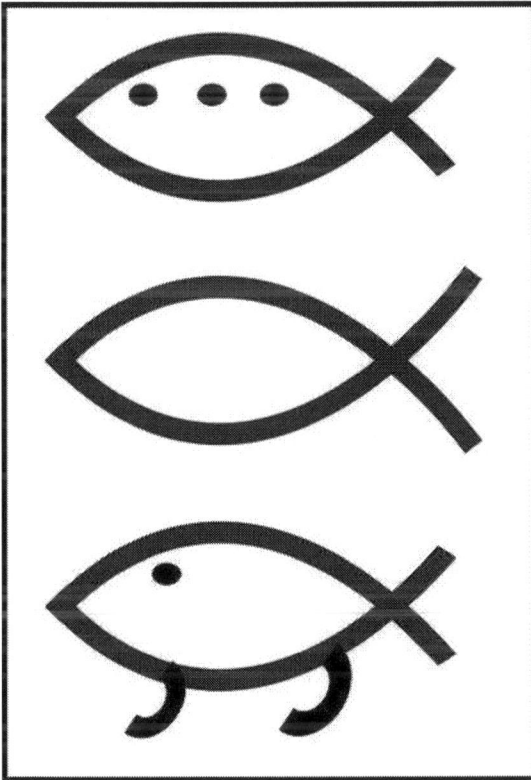

Image 2: Who knows for sure?!

When our ancestors were all hunter gatherers and being chased by some damn scary predators such as sabre-toothed tigers and giant hyenas; remembering the exact details with crystal clarity of how you avoided almost certain death would definitely come in handy. If you didn't learn, you never passed on your genes to the next generation and your lineage ended. We have evolved from, and haves the genes of the smart ones, but as we know, anything valuable usually comes with a hefty price tag.

Even though the potential for death is a constant shadow following each person in their normal activities, most people do not encounter the level of threat our ancestors did on a daily basis. Although we know this at a logical level, our bodies do not have this same understanding and are prewired to respond in certain ways to distressing stimuli whether it is something as simple as merely being late for work, or the real life threat of an IED explosion. Technology - especially weapons - in the last 100 years has evolved far quicker than our species ever could. So now we have all manner of new and terrifying ways of creating traumatic events.

There are a number of possible explanations for why PTSD occurs:

Psychological

When we are frightened, we remember things with extreme clarity. Although it can be distressing to remember these things, it can also help us to understand what happened and provide useful keys to future survival. The recollections make us give some serious contemplation to what happened. We can think about what to do if it should ever happen to us again. By being vigilant we can react quicker if another similar predicament occurs. However we don't want to spend the rest of our life going over it again and again and again and again and again and again and again and again and again, ad infinitum. We only really need to think about it when we have to; this being to prevent a similar occurrence from happening to us in the present moment.

Physical

Adrenaline is just one of the hormones our bodies produce when we are under stress. It prepares the body for action; the good old fight or flight response. In this state, many of your body's normal functions temporarily slow or shut down, such as digestion. After all there's no need to concern yourself with digesting your breakfast when you've got a bear sized hyena on your ass; they'll digest it for you, if you don't either escape or kill him (or her)!

When the danger disappears, levels of adrenaline should go back to normal. When we are in highly anxious states such as with PTSD; it is the replaying of the vivid memories of the trauma which keep the levels of adrenaline high. This makes a person tense, irritable, prone to illness, and unable to relax or sleep soundly. The nervous system cannot differentiate between a real event and one that is vividly imagined. Therefore every time you intensely replay the traumatic event in your mind; your nervous system responds as if you are really experiencing the event again. This is why it is imperative to your physical health and all round wellbeing to seek help and not just suffer in silence, "man it out", or pretend it isn't happening.

Chapter 4

What Are The Symptoms Of PTSD?

Remember I mentioned earlier; what you are going through is a normal reaction to abnormal events; this does not mean you are mentally deficient. At least no more or less than the average veteran or serviceman (or woman)!

After any traumatic experience people can feel depressed, guilty, angry, or any number of what are considered negative emotions. As well as these common emotional reactions, there are three main types of symptoms produced by such an experience:

1. Flashbacks & Nightmares

Self-explanatory, but I will give a little detail for the sake of clarity. This is where you find yourself re-living an event over and over again in your mind. This can happen both as a flashback in the day, and as nightmares when asleep. It will seem as though you are living through the experience all over again. It is normally an associated memory and therefore you will not only see what you saw through your own eyes, but will most likely feel the exact emotions you felt, and the physical bodily sensations identical to what you experienced at the time.

A flashback can be triggered by something external in your environment which is associated with the original event. This could be absolutely anything; a movie, a distinct odour, or even a piece of music which reminds you of your traumatic experience. You will often experience an intense physical reaction to these kinds of reminders of the event, such as an increased heart rate, rapid breathing, tense muscles, or sweating profusely.

2. Avoidance & Numbing

It's not exactly pleasurable to re-live your traumatic experience; so you may not want to talk about the event with anyone. Instead you may try to distract yourself by keeping your mind busy and occupied. This could be by completely absorbing yourself in a hobby, work, or simply by playing computer games for hours at a time.

You may start to avoid people and places which remind you of the trauma. You may have erroneous thoughts about your future such as; not expecting to live a regular life span, never getting married, or ever having another fulfilling career.

A coping mechanism for what you're experiencing is to try feeling nothing at all and just become emotionally numb. Although this last sentence sounds a bit like an ex-girlfriend of mine!

3. Hyper Vigilance

You could find you remain on high alert nearly all the time. It's as if you are expecting danger to materialise at any moment, and therefore you will find it almost impossible to relax. Odds are, you will feel extremely anxious much of the time, and more than likely suffer from insomnia.

People around you will notice you have become edgy, short-tempered, and prone to aggressive outbursts. However, some people – myself included – are naturally like this first thing in the morning!

Other Possible Symptoms

What follows is not an exhaustive list, but merely some possible concerns to consider as indicators:

- Muscular aches and pains
- Migraines or headaches
- Panic/Anxiety attacks
- Depression
- Alcoholism
- Drug Addiction (legal or illegal)
- Extreme mood swings
- Violent outbursts
- Diarrhoea

- Sexual Fetishes

To be fair, most of us who have served could be considered to have a bit of an extreme relationship with alcohol, but you will know the difference between a good "bevvy up" and alcoholism. If you need a drink before you can even function, this may be a good indicator.

Also I met many a Matelot with some weird sexual fantasies, but none of these were what would be considered too unhealthy; although I'm not too sure about Dinga!

Chapter 5

Ways To Tell If You Could Be Suffering From PTSD

The following are just some possible indicators of PTSD, but do not necessarily mean that you are suffering from it. However, if you are exhibiting any of these behaviours during, or after a deployment; then I recommend consulting the "scab-lifters" anyway.

- You have extremely vivid flashbacks and nightmares.
- You avoid people/places which remind you of an event.
- You feel emotionally numb.
- You drink large amounts of alcohol (normal runs ashore don't count.)
- You have a drug habit.
- You suffer from mood swings for no apparent reason.
- You find it difficult to get on with other people.
- You have to keep busy all the time to distract yourself.
- You feel irritable and constantly edgy.
- You are easily fatigued.
- You feel depressed.

If it is less that 6 weeks since the traumatic event and these kinds of symptoms are improving, then this may be part of the normal process of getting over it. However, if it is more than 6 weeks since the event, and these experiences don't seem to be getting any better, I advise you to definitely contact your doctor before seeking any kind of "complimentary" treatment. Of course the choice is always yours.

With the amount of time troops are spending in theatre during their service, it may not be until after leaving the forces, your symptoms become apparent. During this transition time is when you will be most vulnerable. Listening to some armchair critics opinion, reading about some minority group showing you contempt in the media, or even your partner's inability to truly empathise can be enough to set off a flashback which leads you to do something you later regret.

Remember: You are highly trained and skilled in the art of warfare. If you use those skills in Civvy Street you will go to prison, PTSD will probably not be an adequate defence. I personally met an Ex-Soldier who was sentenced to 6 years in Prison. He served in Iraq and one night in his hometown, some scumbag pulled a knife on him. In his words "I kicked the fuck out of him!"

Fine, you can't go round beating people up and expect to get away with it, but at the same time; what do they expect to happen if you just leave combat troops to fend for themselves without any real transitional support and advice?

Chapter 6

Stress, Anxiety & Depression

Image 3: I'd be stressed too with all those words following me!

<u>Ordinary Stress</u>

We need a certain amount of stress in our lives, otherwise we would all just lie around all day doing diddly-squat; because there would be no pressure to get out of bed, cook and eat food, or go to work. Stress is part of normal, everyday life, but can also produce anxiety, depression, anger, tiredness, and headaches.

Nearly everybody feels overly stressed from time to time. However, our response to stress is entirely subjective: it is just an emotional reaction to everyday events. These events could be connected with work, relationships, or money, etc. We get angry, sad, and anxious about things which are totally outside of our control. We become emotional over "what is" as if by shouting, worrying or crying; it will change events so we can get our own way. Let's face it, if there was something we could do about the situation there and then; we'd do it!

Stress can also make some physical problems worse, such as stomach ulcers, raised blood pressure and skin conditions. It is said, stress is the biggest killer in the Western World. As it is not an event, but our reaction to an event which causes "stress", I would go as far as to say most ill health is caused by ordinary subjective stress. This is based on recent findings and research, but I don't wish to overload you with heavy theories too early in this book! This kind of stress is not the same as PTSD.

Anxiety

Anxiety as described in one dictionary I used when writing my original PDF guide - which for the life of me I can't find again - is "a psychological and physiological state characterized by cognitive, somatic, emotional, and behavioural components.

These components combine to create an unpleasant feeling that is typically associated with uneasiness, fear, or worry."

I personally believe ALL negative human emotions have their basis in FEAR at some level. Underpinning most destructive behaviours is fear, which could also be described as the absence of a feeling of love and security in the moment. We feel the physical effects of fear/anxiety in the present moment, yet the mind is not in this same present moment. It could be in the future imagining an unpleasant occurrence it believes is going to happen, or it could be in the past remembering shameful feelings of guilt.

Clearly there are times to feel fear; when there is some direct and imminent threat to our wellbeing. However, most anxiety is caused by repeatedly imagining future events; which never actually happen. Statistically speaking, only around 3% of our worries ever come true.

Symptoms of anxiety are numerous and take many forms such as phobias, O.C.D., nerve rashes, addictions and many more. I would estimate that 95% of my clients when I was offering one-to-one consultations suffered from anxiety related issues, and therefore I devoted many years to discovering the multitude of causes for this emotion, and the fastest most effective treatments for anxiety reduction.

Despite all this knowledge, I am not immune to the odd bout of pointless worry every now and again. But when I catch myself wasting my emotional energy in this way, I can usually snap my thoughts back to what is happening in the moment I am actually in. Later in this book, I will share a thought exercise I used to use in my consultation room to demonstrate exactly how pointless worry really is.

<u>Depression</u>

There are many causes for depression, and it is not my purpose in this book to offer advice for those suffering from bi-polar or any other forms of clinical depression. Once again, please go and visit your Doctor.

Side Note (Tangent): I'm starting to sound like a stuck record, I know; but the more I repeat it, the less likely someone is going to claim my book turned them into a shrubbery shagger. As if they weren't one in the first place! Sorry, I'm going off on one of my famous digressions now, but these people who are looking to blame someone else for everything which is not right in their life do annoy me; but only a little bit. OK, minor rant over, let's get back on track.

Anything from a slightly low mood to long lasting sadness could be considered a form of depression. Symptoms will vary from person to person and we just haven't got the time to go into detail here. For some (not all), thoughts of, or even actual attempts at suicide are a cry for help because they feel there is no one in the world who gives a flying toss about them; and they want to see if they are right.

I think the following line from the song "Nowhere Fast" by "The Smiths" sums up depression rather well and probably is the closest thing you'll get to a general all-encompassing statement of what you often feel like:

"And when I'm lying in my bed, I think about life & I think about death; and neither one particularly appeals to me."

I personally experienced this sort of emotional state back in 2002 when in the space of about 4 days and totally unexpectedly, my whole world seemed to fold in on itself. I won't go into too much graphic detail, but here's a brief summary:

1. The mate I shared a house with decided to move out, which resulted in my outgoings doubling.
2. I contracted Hepatitis 'A' from cleaning toilets in the part-time job I had at the time. I didn't actually know this during these first few days of hell. I just knew something was seriously wrong when I couldn't keep down any solids or liquids, and lost 3 Stone in weight rapidly. It took numerous blood tests over about 5 weeks to discover the correct diagnosis.

   But I digress, the result of this illness was I obviously couldn't work with clients, received a pittance of sick pay from my part-time job, and so had to survive off credit cards for 6 months.

3. The final nail in the coffin was when my girlfriend at the time came round to tell me she had slept with someone else. On its own this wouldn't have been a real biggy - I haven't exactly lived the life of a Saint - but in conjunction with the previous two occurrences; it pushed me over the edge.

There were a few other lesser disasters which appeared during this time, but these three were the main crux of my misery. This was probably the darkest period of my life in some ways, but in others it was quite an enlightening and creative time. Though I had never really written much before, I wrote an absolute bucket load of poetry during this time. Some of it was very, very dark, some was poignant or philosophical in nature, and a few were just plain embarrassing or silly.

After a while, there were even moments when I started to enjoy the things which were going wrong; as they provided inspiration for more prose!

On the next page is quite a dark example, and was actually the thirteenth one I wrote...

The Thirteenth Verse

As I slip the rope around my neck,
I pause a moment to reflect:
Is it worth the pain I'll cause,
To the one who will open the doors?

Jump with weights into the sea,
To be found then, most unlikely.
Closer still, a closed mine shaft?
A shotgun? No, that's daft.

Perhaps an overdose will do.
No, be original, try something new.
Climb into the freezer box,
Close the lid, so it locks.

Now I think about it again,
There's a nagging thought within my brain.
Suicide is too easy a way out.
So no more, shall I ever doubt.

Life's worth living even with the pain.
Even if it sends me quite insane.
Perhaps I'm in my own personal hell.
I guess; that only time will tell.

Once I was over the worst of the hepatitis - around 6 weeks - I briefly took medication for my depression. After a week or two I realised, or maybe remembered, I could pull myself out of the doldrums with my knowledge and experience. I don't recommend coming off medication if you have been prescribed it, because there can be adverse side-effects if you reduce too quickly. In my case, I don't think they'd had time to kick in properly, maybe I was just lucky, or perhaps my writing style is one of those side-effects!

I share this story and the poem with you for a few reasons: Firstly to show everyone, even therapists go through some really shit times in their lives. Secondly to show there is indeed life after depression. But thirdly and probably more importantly, if you ever find there is no one to share how you feel with, get creative. It doesn't matter what medium you use; paint, sculpture or just the written word in any of its forms. If you express your pain in one of these ways, you will have essentially gotten "things off your chest". It may not work for everyone, but after personal experience of this kind of catharsis, I shared this idea with many clients who told me it really helped them to cope and eventually feel great again.

Chapter 7

A Few Do's And Do Not's For Self Treatment Of PTSD

Do:

- CONTACT YOUR DOCTOR!!
- Keep life as normal as possible.
- Talk about what happened with a friend or family member who you trust.
- Use relaxation techniques such as Yoga, Tai-chi, self-hypnosis, guided meditation, etc.
- Eat regularly.
- Exercise frequently.
- Spend time with family and friends.
- Expect and more importantly BELIEVE You Will Get Better.
- Research the subject of PTSD, the more you understand about it; the less power it will have over you.
- Smile and Laugh as much as possible. You cannot be happy and depressed at the same time.

Do Not:

- Beat yourself up about it: PTSD symptoms are not a sign of weakness. They are a normal reaction to abnormal experiences.
- Bottle up your feelings.
- Keep it to yourself.
- Avoid talking about it.
- Shut yourself away from other people.
- Drink lots of alcohol, coffee or even smoke more.
- Miss meals.
- Take it out on people, who can never truly understand.
- Be afraid to use "Complimentary" techniques. It's your wellbeing and it isn't the sceptics who are suffering.

In addition to this list, I personally recommend avoiding main stream media in all its formats. Believe me; you will still know what is happening in the world, only you will not be overwhelmed with "doom and gloom".

Section 2: Treatments For PTSD

FIRSTLY, I SAY AGAIN: VISIT YOUR DOCTOR!
Most effective treatments for PTSD involve helping you to deal
with the trauma you've experienced head on. Instead of avoiding
the trauma or anything which reminds you of it, you'll be asked
to recall and process the emotions and sensations you felt during
the original event during the treatment. By offering a channel for
the emotions you may have bottled up to be released; it will help
to re-establish a sense of control and diminish the grip the
memory of the trauma has had on you.

If you were coming to see me when I was in practice, the
course of treatment I offered would be catered to your individual
specific circumstances; and so what follows is merely a rough
outline. However, because E.F.T. appears to be especially
effective and relatively speedy in dealing with PTSD, I have
dedicated an entire section of this book to this discipline, because
it is the technique which will be easiest to self-administer,
without the need for months, or years of study.

I will provide you with an outline of the treatments which I
used in my Consultation Room and others I have done a little
research on, in case you are considering visiting someone who
offers a similar or alternative service. I say similar, because no
one can offer you the same service I used to. This is not ego, just

simply the fact, no other Practitioner has had my personal life experiences, studied exactly the same books and courses, and attended the same workshops; and so they too will – or should - offer their own unique service.

Chapter 8

Hypnotherapy

Hypnotherapy is a drug-free method of deep relaxation where the clients' unconscious mind becomes more open to positive suggestions. It is a totally natural and safe state, induced by the therapist, with the client always remaining in control. You cannot be made to say or do anything against your will. If you wished to terminate a session at any point, you would be free to do so.

Anybody over the age of about 6, not strongly under the influence of drugs or alcohol, and with a full mental capability is able to go into the hypnotic state if they choose to. The hypnotic experience can vary from person to person, and from session to session. Here is a list of some of the ways you could feel during a session:

- You may be aware of feeling like you are floating.
- You may feel heavy and unable to move.
- You may start flushing up, or start feeling cool.
- You may get "pins and needles".
- It can feel like you're in a lucid dream.
- Or it may just feel like you've got your eyes closed and you're just listening to someone waffling on!

However you experience hypnosis is irrelevant to the success of a treatment. Hypnosis has a very high rate of success in removing problems on its own or can speed up the process when used in conjunction with other treatments.

Hypnotherapy can be split into two main categories…

<u>Suggestion Therapy</u>

Similar to what you have probably seen with stage show hypnosis. Only a therapist is not going to get you to bark like a dog, cluck like a chicken, or shag a shrubbery!

Image 4: Look into the eyes, the eyes…

When I was working as a Consultant, if you came to see me as a client, you would be made comfortable, with some relaxing music playing. Then I would ask you to close your eyes for the duration of the actual Hypnosis session. I would proceed to give you some positive suggestions to help you to drift into a deeply relaxing hypnotic trance. You would still be aware of your surroundings; it said you are more aware when you are in the state of hypnosis. When I saw you were suitably relaxed, I would give you precise suggestions to take care of your specific concerns. Each suggestion would have been carefully checked for any ambiguity, something which stage show hypnotists sometimes fall foul of.

I personally would not use suggestion therapy alone to remove PTSD symptoms. I would only consider using this style of hypnosis as a relaxation technique for a client who is extremely tense, and maybe to work on some specific anxiety symptoms. Other Hypnotherapists may disagree and it is their free choice to do so.

Analytical Hypnotherapy

This is used for the treatment of more deep-rooted problems, by searching for the originating cause. Much of my early training and studies were centred on the theories of Sigmund Freud, and therefore this was my preferred style of treatment for many years. Eventually I got round to reading some of Carl Jung's work, before moving on to all kinds of studies. As I did this, I became less reliant on psycho-analysis, and I guess worked more on instinct with what I believed would be best for the client. However, it was still very effective for those who saw the analysis through to the end, and many people still use it. So I'll rewind time and give a short explanation of how I did things back in the day.

In some cases a repressed memory is responsible for causing us symptoms. Unlike a disavowal where we just choose to deny an event has taken place; a repressed memory is one which we have no conscious recollection of. This is caused by an event which is so traumatic; the mind locks it away so we never have to think about it again. An example of a supposed repressed memory is being born. Not many people can recall this first slap on the arse. You have to agree, after the cosiness of the womb, coming out to experience the big bad world has to qualify as a major trauma, doesn't it?!

If you should choose this method of treatment to help with your PTSD, you would be relaxed in the same manner as "Suggestion Therapy". Then you would be regressed back through periods of your life connected to your concern. You as the client will be doing most of the talking. By using free association, you will be linking and connecting one memory to another, and sharing any emotions you feel connected with your recalls. Eventually all your troubles from youth can be discarded until only the repressed one remains. To find this trauma usually involves a greater number of sessions. The use of hypnosis will speed up the discovery of the originating cause, and 6 - 8 sessions are normally required (without hypnosis, it can take years).

The original cause of why you're suffering from PTSD could be connected to an event from your childhood, or even a past life experience. Once the recollection of this originating cause comes into conscious awareness, it can be dealt with, and like any other memory; eventually forgotten about.

Note: Whether people actually come back in another body or not, obviously cannot be proved one way or the other. However there is plenty of evidence to suggest people who believe they have been here before have gotten over symptoms when regressed to these "past lives".

Hypnosis At Home

I just want to assure you, if you do any kind of hypnosis at home; you cannot get stuck in the hypnotic state indefinitely, despite what you may have seen in some horror films. The worse thing which could happen is, you would eventually drift off into a natural sleep and wake up of your own accord.

On one of the first pages of my diploma course was this description: "Hypnosis is a deep relaxation and a focusing of the mind." So technically speaking, if you are comfortable and engrossed in this book right now; you are in a state of hypnosis.

There are a few good books available which I have read on the subject of self-hypnosis, if you wish to look into the topic for yourself. If this is not for you, then you can always purchase a CD from a reputable source. I have a few I recorded in 2010 on my own website available - which do come with a full money back guarantee - if you struggle to find any. However I must point out, there is only a limited range, because as I have already mentioned, I have taken a break from therapy to work on other projects.

In a moment I'm going to share a short relaxation script which I've created especially for you, so you don't even need to buy a CD. But first I need to give a few instructions on how to get maximum benefit from it.

Back when I first qualified in Hypnotherapy, if I wanted to record a Hypnosis cassette tape, yes a "cassette tape", I would either have to hire a recording studio – which was not an option – or do the following routine:

1. Play hypnotic music at maximum level on the main stereo in my house.
2. Record the session on a portable cassette player with only a built in microphone.
3. Attempt to speak with a calm soothing tone, even though I could not hear my own voice.
4. Hope no one telephoned, knocked on the door, or made any other kind of disturbance.

5. Hope I didn't make any kind of mistake, because I'd have to start from the beginning again.

It could take a few days to record just one forty minute tape. Though, I must say, they didn't sound too bad for the time when done. Nowadays, it is an absolute doddle to record your own stuff extremely cheaply. All you need is your computer, a microphone, and some editing software. For my Hypnosis CDs, I bought some Royalty Free music, a fairly expensive microphone, and use "Audacity" software for editing. I know some people prefer to use "Sound Forge", but I've chosen to stick with the first one I came across and can get by using.

The time consuming part of the process is writing the script, and to me this is the enjoyable part. So seeing how I've provided the following example script for you, all you will need to do is record it if you choose to, and put some soothing music in the background, and anything will do for this exercise.

If you do choose to do it, simply speak in a slow, almost monotonous tone, leaving bigger pauses between words than in normal conversation and you should have an adequate session to use to help you to relax. It is only for your own personal use, so do not worry about it sounding professional.

If you don't think listening to your own voice will be able to relax you, you'll just have to take my word for it, you can. I used to cringe when I first heard my voice on a recording, but now I have no problem with it whatsoever, and often listen to programs I have created for personal use.

One warning: never play any kind of hypnotic or relaxation program whilst driving, or operating any kind or machinery. Especially do not play them whilst on duty, the potential consequences don't bear thinking about.

If you are planning on playing your recording and need to do something afterwards, it might be an idea to set an alarm to go off about 10 minutes after it is due to finish, just in case you do drift off to sleep. If you do have any concerns, you could always get a trusted friend to read it to you first.

When you play your recording, find somewhere comfortable to lie down on your back, arms by your side, and put a pillow under your head. It's OK to fidget or scratch if you need to whilst you are listening to it.

This script is not for times when you are exhibiting any of your strong PTSD symptoms, but rather as a relaxation and confidence boost when you are feeling reasonably fine.

In the following script any words in (parentheses) are actions and not to be read out, everything else between the "inverted commas" is to be spoken, and any words which are <u>underlined</u> you can give an emphasis to as you say them.

Relaxation & Confidence Script

"I just want you to get yourself comfortable whilst I'm talking, so it really doesn't matter whether you focus on the words I'm saying, or just allow your mind to absorb them naturally and unconsciously, just as easily as you can feel your head touching the pillow.

(Pause for 10 seconds.)

Just as you can hear the words I'm saying to you, and feel yourself becoming more relaxed; you can allow your eyes to gently close now if they haven't already.

It's okay if you need to fidget or scratch or alter position whilst listening to my voice whilst you drift off into a calming and peaceful kind of state.

(Pause for 10 seconds.)

I would like you now to begin focusing on your breathing.

Notice the rhythm as you become much more relaxed.

Just imagine every time you breathe in that you are filling every nerve, every fibre and every cell of your body with a calming energy.

And every time you breathe out; you are breathing away any remaining tension.

(Pause for 10 seconds.)

In a moment we're going to go deeper into relaxation and it's okay if you stop paying attention to the actual words I'm saying.

And if you do, you will come out of this relaxation at the end of this recording (or you can say "session"), feeling refreshed, invigorated and ready to move forward in pursuit of your goals. All the positive suggestions that I am going to give to you will be absorbed by your mind, and acted upon whether you pay attention to the words consciously or unconsciously, because you know they are all for your higher good.

So right now, as you focus on your breathing, I'd like you to take a deep breath in and then allow any last bits of tension to completely disappear as you breathe out. That's good.

(Pause for 10 seconds.)

Just allow your focus to shift to the tiny muscles in your face; around your eyes, your nose, and your mouth.

Focus on these muscles and allow them to relax.

And you will find as you listen to me speak, and focus on your breathing; this relaxation will be spreading through your entire body, more and more.

Spreading down through your neck and out into your shoulders, down your arms, through your wrists, into your hands, and out through the fingers.

And as you feel this relaxation in your arms, you can also notice it spreading down your spine and into your thighs; relaxing your chest, back, and abdomen on the way.

And as you feel the relaxation passing through your knees and down your calves and towards your feet and toes you may notice that your body feels kind of floaty; and whether it does or does not; this is perfectly fine.

(Pause for 20 seconds.)

Notice how much more relaxed, and calm, and peaceful you are feeling already.

That's good, as relaxed as you can be in this present moment, ready to imagine, and ready to absorb the positive suggestions you are about to hear.

The things that could once upset you will now simply calm and relax you.

(Pause from 30 seconds up to five minutes, depending on how long you want the recording to last).)

I'd like you now to contemplate the following:

You were born with a genetic template for confidence and success.

Your ancestors, as far back as you care to imagine, were highly successful survivors. If they were not, you would not be here, listening to these words, right now.

Generation after generation have passed on these strong, confident, successful traits through their genes.

Thousands of years of success strategies have been honed to perfection, and you are the result of all that success.

(Pause for 20 seconds.)

At the Quantum level, you are the universe. So no matter your personal beliefs, you have the same power within you as a star, a lion, a mountain, or anything you care to imagine.

You were born with all the tools you require to <u>be successful</u>.

Your unconscious mind can process more information than any computer.

It is the ultimate problem solver.

Focus on the outcomes you desire and it will present you with a way to manifest them.

All you need to do is: <u>believe in yourself</u>.

(Pause for 20 seconds.)

I would like you to begin to focus your attention on all your strengths, both inner and outer.

Allow all worries and anxieties to disappear or just fade away, they simply fade away.

(Pause for 30 seconds.)

From this day forth:

You will feel much more <u>confident</u> in your decisions.

You will feel much more <u>confidence</u> in your actions.

You will exhibit much more <u>confidence</u> in the presence of other people, whether they are strangers or people with whom you are already acquainted.

(Pause for 20 seconds.)

I want you to eliminate from your vocabulary such words as; try, should, can't, etc., and replace them with:

It is a certainty that I am bound to succeed. Any setbacks are valuable lessons from which I shall learn and grow.

I am solely in control of my destiny.

Give me any problem, and I will always find a solution.

(Pause for 10 seconds.)

Remember: always expect that something good is going to happen, something better. But for now, just relax, relax, relax.

(Pause for 20 seconds.)

In a moment, I will be bringing this session to an end by counting up to 10, and when I reach 10, you will open your eyes, wide awake, and feeling wonderful.

Here we go:

1. Bringing your thoughts back to the room you are currently in.
2. Becoming aware of your surroundings.
3. Feeling relaxed and refreshed.
4. Starting to really notice other sounds in your environment.
5. Really becoming aware of the room you are in.
6. Feeling totally energised.
7. Eyes are beginning to open now; mind and body returning to normality.
8. That's it, eyes starting to open now.
9. Totally invigorated, refreshed and totally aware of your surroundings and …
10. Eyes wide open now, that's it, eyes wide open, and completely at peace, but totally revitalised and ready to carry on with your day.

Your mind and body returned to normality"

I created this script especially for this book, but feel free to alter any words you feel uncomfortable with if you plan on recording it. The only part I wouldn't alter is the count to ten at the end.

Although if done correctly by a trained professional, this script would be adequate to get you into a proper deep hypnotic trance, it will really be more of a guided meditation or relaxation if you should choose to record it following these instructions.

Chapter 9

Neuro-Linguistic Programming

N.L.P. has been defined as "The study of the structure of our subjective experience and what can be calculated from it." In other words, how we communicate with ourselves can be in error. A classic saying used by N.L.P. practitioners is "The Map is not the territory." Simply put, our view of reality based on subjective experience is not necessarily a true depiction of how things really are.

There are various techniques used to change thought patterns to improve the way we interact with the world and how we view it. Some of these techniques will work very well with changing certain PTSD symptoms.

Although I may have used some N.L.P. in the course of treatment, I rarely conducted purely N.L.P. sessions with paying clients. I admit; it was one area where I didn't keep up to date with all the latest techniques, because initially I wasn't the biggest fan of N.L.P. when I first qualified in this discipline back in 1998. Over the last couple of years though, I have been hearing good things about it from attending seminars; so maybe I should have given the subject more attention after all! I have bought a few books to revisit the subject in greater detail when I have some spare study time.

If you are interested in learning more about this subject I recommend you research the founders: Richard Bandler & John Grinder.

I'll share one quick and simple technique which I still use when someone talks about some negative situation they find themselves in. You know the kind of thing I'm talking about; you're having a great day and then someone has to ruin it by going on a dripping session.

It may sound like something from this list:

- "I can't believe he/she did that again."
- "It really gets on my tits when he/she does that."
- "They always keep treating me like this."

(For he/she/they insert a person's name, & for this/that substitute some sort of behaviour.)

We may not be able to go back in time and change the real event - at least not yet - but how we choose to remember it; we do have some control of. When someone is retelling an event from their lives, they will usually be playing some sort of movie of the experience in their mind. Well the great thing is; we can become director, producer and editor of this movie. We can also be in charge of lighting, Foley, and special effects. In fact, we can become the entire crew for this imaginary flick!

In N.L.P. they call it changing the submodalities of the sensory data in the memory. This in simple English means the qualities of the things we are imagining such as big, small, distant, bright, etc. I think an example is required here for clarity....

Image 5: "Are You Eyeballing Me Boy?!!"

Let's say someone had a RSM who was a particularly harsh son of a bitch. A member of his company happens to take the bollockings to heart, and after a while it begins to get them down.

Every time this RSM's name is mentioned, our poor recruit instantly replays the memory of the most severe of these reprimands in his mind. The memory is associated, which means he sees it through his own eyes, just like when he was actually there. He may recall the smell of the Sergeant's halitosis as he shouted a mere few millimetres from his nose, the brightness of the dormitory lighting which gave the RSM some kind of demonic aura, and the sound of his bellowing causing a ringing in his ears.

One thing we can do is disassociate ourselves from the recall. This means we watch it from another angle and can see ourselves in the movie as one of the performers. When we do this, it will lessen the emotional effect the story has on us. If you find this difficult to do –as I do personally – do not worry, we can now begin to change the submodalities, and I've never encountered a person who couldn't do this. This is an extremely condensed version of the kind of thing I would say to our recruit in our example:

"I want you to play this movie over in your mind again. But this time, imagine the RSM's breath smells of the sweetest perfume you've ever smelt. I also want you to imagine his voice has gone up in pitch several octaves and he now sounds like a choirboy. And whilst we are at it, I'd like you to imagine he has sprouted some Angel Wings and the light behind him is actually emanating from a halo above his head. Now run through this movie again,

but move yourself further back from the Sergeant, so he appears smaller."

Depending on how well the person was imagining what I was describing would determine how much more tweaking we would need to do. We could play the movie in black and white, slow-motion, fast forward/rewind, or even shrink the RSM down to the size of an ant. You can change absolutely any aspect of the movie; you are only limited by your imagination. The idea is to erase the old movie by replaying the new version over and over until it is the only one which springs to mind, and then be able to think of the memory without any negative emotion coming up.

You can try this yourself with a memory which is not too distressing, or just do it with a person who gets on your nerves. Simply see them wearing something silly like flippers and a tutu. Turn their voice in to a sound rather than words and then move this sound up or down a few octaves. Get them doing some sort of silly behaviour which would be out of character for them, such as breakdancing and voila; you'll piss yourself laughing every time you think about them.

Chapter 10
Other Treatments

There may well be other "Complimentary Treatments" which can help with PTSD, but as I have either not studied them at great depth or tried them personally; I will not and cannot comment on their effectiveness in regards to removing the symptoms of PTSD. Disciplines such as stress massage, acupuncture, reflexology, etc. may help in dealing with symptoms in the short term, but I doubt they would provide long term resolution for you.

Being something of a perfectionist, I would take it personally quite hard if I failed to rid a client of their problem permanently. Even though my overall success rate in my 13 years of practice was around 90% (apparently most people average around 70-80%), I always felt like a failure and a fraud when results were not what I had expected.

Having worked in a Natural Health Centre for 11 years which went from only having around 8 different disciplines in the beginning to around 30 before I left; I will offer these personal observations:

- Many Therapists are in need of therapy more than their clients (me included, though you may have been thinking this already!).
- Some treatments offer only temporary relief of symptoms and not a cure.
- Some treatments require you to come month after month, year after year.
- Some therapists are only interested in promoting their own discipline and will not recommend alternative treatments, even when they are more effective for certain conditions.
- Some "new" treatments seem to be made up for people who have "more money than sense"!
- Some people become Therapists to make money only. As long as you pay the fee, they are not really bothered whether you get better or not.

Do not let any of this put you off exploring such treatments. If you find relief from your symptoms, or even better "a cure"; then this is all that matters.

For the sake of completion I have done a little digging around and found a few treatments which are considered to be effective in managing the symptoms of PTSD. You may want to consider trying:

Eye Movement Desensitization and Reprocessing (EMDR)

This is a technique which uses eye movements to help the brain to process flashbacks and make sense of a traumatic experience. Though I have never worked with any therapist who actually practices this type of therapy; I have heard it can be very effective. I was at one time considering studying the subject myself after completing my qualifications in E.F.T. So what follows is only a very brief introduction to the subject.

The American Psychologist Francine Shapiro is the originator of EMDR, which is a form of psychotherapy developed to resolve the development of trauma-related disorders resulting from experiencing a harrowing event such as assault, rape or military conflict. Although some consultants use EMDR for other problems, its research is primarily for conditions associated with disturbing life experiences. It uses a structured eight-phase approach and addresses the past, present, and future aspects of the dysfunctional memory. During this process, the client focuses on short periods of the traumatic memory in multiple sets of about 15–30 seconds, while simultaneously focusing on a dual attention stimulus. This could be lateral eye movements directed by the therapist, alternate hand-tapping or bilateral auditory tones. After each set of dual attention stimuli, the patient will be asked to describe what associative information was produced, and this usually becomes the focus of the next set. The process of alternating dual attention and personal association is continual throughout a consultation.

EMDR is thought to work by unfreezing the brain's data processing system, which has been interrupted by extreme stress. This stress leaves only frozen emotional fragments of the experience along with their original intensity. Once these fragments are freed of the emotional distress, they can be integrated into a solid memory and managed.

Cognitive Behavioural Therapies (CBT)

From the limited research I have done to date on CBT, it appears to be a highly recommended treatment in the U.K. for some mental health conditions, such as OCD, bulimia nervosa, clinical depression and also PTSD.

CBT is a psychotherapeutic talking therapy, which can help to understand how "habits of thinking" can make PTSD worse, or even cause it. The objective is to "eradicate problems relating to dysfunctional emotions, behaviours and thoughts through a goal-oriented, systematic procedure". In other words it aims to help you to change these ways of thinking, which will help you to feel better and to behave differently, but then again, so do most flavours of psychotherapy!

CBT is used in both individual therapy and in group settings, and the techniques are often adapted for self-help applications. Some therapists will be more cognitive oriented and use cognitive restructuring techniques, whilst others will be more behaviourally oriented using in vivo exposure therapy; i.e. real life confrontation with triggers such as people, places, and objects. Of course there will also be those who will use a combination of both; with imaginary exposure therapy techniques.

Group Therapy

There are many groups forming to help sufferers of PTSD. The number one benefit of attending - as I see it - is you will be in the company of a peer group who can fully empathise with the emotional strains you are experiencing.

I will conclude this section with a little information on the "12 Step Program" which was first created to help people suffering with alcoholism in 1935 by Bill Wilson. They have since gone on to be formed to help with all manner of addictive behaviours, and also emotional traumas. I did a quick search on the internet, and lo and behold; there are programs of this nature being set up to deal specifically with PTSD.

I found the following information on Wikipedia about "12 Step Programs", so cannot say how factually correct it is, but thought I'd include it so you know what is involved, should you consider attending. Maybe not everyone's cup of tea, but it will be of benefit for some who read this book.

For the sake of space I have edited slightly what I found:

The Twelve Steps

These are the original Twelve Steps as published by Alcoholics Anonymous:

- We admitted we were powerless over alcohol, our lives had become unmanageable.
- Came to believe a Power greater than ourselves could restore us to sanity.
- Made a decision to turn our will and our lives over to the care of God as we understood Him.
- Made a searching and fearless moral inventory of ourselves.
- Admitted to God, to ourselves, and to another human being the exact nature of our wrongs.
- Were entirely ready to have God remove all these defects of character.
- Humbly asked Him to remove our shortcomings.
- Made a list of all persons we had harmed, and became willing to make amends to them all.
- Made direct amends to such people wherever possible, except when to do so would injure them or others.
- Continued to take personal inventory and when we were wrong promptly admitted it.

- Sought through prayer and meditation to improve our conscious contact with God as we understood Him, praying only for knowledge of His will for us and the power to carry that out.
- Having had a spiritual awakening as the result of these steps, we tried to carry this message to alcoholics, and to practice these principles in all our affairs.

Twelve Traditions

The Twelve Traditions accompany the Twelve Steps. The Traditions provide guidelines for group governance. They were developed in AA in order to help resolve conflicts in the areas of publicity, religion and finances. Most twelve-step fellowships have adopted these principles for their structural governance. The Twelve Traditions of Alcoholics Anonymous are as follows:

- Our common welfare should come first; personal recovery depends upon unity.
- For our group purpose there is but one ultimate authority, a loving God as He may express Himself in our group conscience. Our leaders are but trusted servants; they do not govern.
- The only requirement for membership is a desire to stop drinking (or other behaviour)

- Each group should be autonomous except in matters affecting other groups.
- Each group has but one primary purpose; to carry its message to the person who still suffers.
- A group ought never endorse, finance, or lend the (group) name to any related facility or outside enterprise, lest problems of money, property, and prestige divert us from our primary purpose.
- Every group ought to be fully self-supporting, declining outside contributions.
- The group should remain forever non-professional, but our service centres may employ special workers.
- The group, as such, ought never to be organized; but we may create service boards or committees directly responsible to those they serve.
- The group has no opinion on outside issues; hence the (group) name ought never to be drawn into public controversy.
- Our public relations policy is based on attraction rather than promotion; we need always maintain personal anonymity at the level of press, radio, and films.
- Anonymity is the spiritual foundation of all our traditions, ever reminding us to place principles before personalities.

This concludes Section 2, and I hope it has given you some possible avenues to explore either now or at a future time. In the next section we will cover the best, and easiest to self-administer technique I have found to date; Emotional Freedom Techniques. There is a similar therapy based on the same principle of tapping on energy meridians called Thought Field Therapy (TFT), which was developed by an American Psychologist, Dr Roger Callahan. However I didn't see the point in doing a write up on it, when it takes longer – and more money – to train in the discipline. If you like what follows on EFT, you can always research TFT for yourself.

Section 3: EFT For PTSD

In this section I am going to teach you the very basics of EFT so you can help yourself. There is much more to EFT than I can cover, because there are many more techniques; some of which I haven't even done the training for.

It will probably also help you, if you watch the videos I created, in conjunction with this guide until you are fully acquainted with the method. You can find them by visiting this link:

www.youtube.com/user/skilledexforces

If you find what is included here helpful, you can always go on to do the training yourself or look up the work of the founder of EFT, Gary Craig. I have seen videos of Gary helping Vietnam Veterans who suffered from PTSD and had been receiving treatment for over 40 years. Clearly people only share their success stories; however it was evident he was very successful with the ones I saw.

Although I have never read it, I discovered whilst researching for a title for this book, Gary has a book entitled "EFT for PTSD". So if you want to get an even deeper look at the subject, I would imagine this would be the next book to buy. And no, I'm not on commission!

Chapter 11

Why I'm Impressed By EFT

As I said earlier in the book; I was sceptical about E.F.T. when I booked to go on the Training Course. I had heard a lot of good things about it from some high profile and reputable sources; so felt I should at least approach it with an open mind; as I endeavour to approach most things.

As we learned the techniques, we would have a brief practice on each other whilst the tutors watched and offered advice. It was during one of these practices during my Level 2 training that I worked with a lady who had a fear of heights. We were in a hotel, about 6 or 7 floors up. As you may recall, I'm not exactly the biggest fan of heights myself. I remembered, during my Level 1 training I had been slightly reluctant to look out of the window of the room. After a bit of "tapping" I had been quite comfortable doing this simple task. I decided to use the same scenario with the lady I was working with. She was far worse than ever I was. She wouldn't even go near the window, never mind look out of it. I only worked with her for about 5 minutes, and was amazed when we both looked out of the "open" window and she exhibited no anxiety symptoms whatsoever. OK, she would need more work to get over her fear completely (as do I), but to make such a leap in ability to face a fear, in such a short time, made me realise how powerful EFT really is.

Although, I would rarely use "Suggestion Therapy" for a fear of heights; on occasion I would, but this would still usually require at least 2 or 3 full sessions. "Analytical Therapy" would normally require around 6 - 8 sessions, although I did get someone over this same fear in only 2 sessions once. N.L.P. has been known to remove phobias in a single session, but as I mentioned earlier, at the time I wasn't convinced about its long term effectiveness. (This was due to something called symptom substitution for those interested in my reasoning.)

Here was a simple, quick and apparently effective technique which really seemed to work; I sat up and paid much more attention than I thought I was going to!

Chapter 12

Frequently Asked Questions

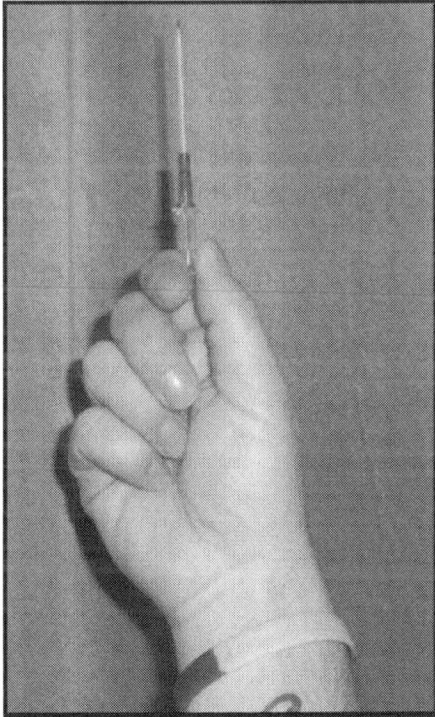

Image 6: Fortunately, no needles required!

What is EFT?

EFT was developed by Gary Craig and has its roots in ancient
Chinese medicine and the modern science of Applied
Kinesiology. According to the basic theory of EFT; the cause of
all negative emotions is a disruption in the body's energy system

or meridians as they are known. EFT aims to restore the bodies' natural balance by removing the energy disruption and thus eliminating the problem.

You may be pleased to know; unlike acupuncture EFT does not use needles! EFT relieves the symptoms by a weird looking system of tapping with the fingertips on specific points on the energy meridians. No one knows for sure why some pain and physical problems respond to EFT in the same way as emotional problems, but they often do.

Do you have to believe in EFT for it to work?

Not at all; I was very sceptical when I went on the training course. EFT works whether you believe in it or not. It doesn't even matter if the practitioner believes in it or not. It will either work for you or it won't; and it usually does!

What can be treated using EFT?

Experienced EFT Practitioners say to use this technique on anything; you have nothing to lose by giving it a go. These techniques have been used successfully by thousands of people with a broad range of difficulties including:

- Addictions
- Allergies

- Anxiety and Panic Attacks
- Anger management
- Obsession Compulsive Disorders
- Depression and Sorrow
- Dyslexia
- Guilt
- Insomnia
- Jealousy
- Nightmares
- Pain Management
- Physical Conditions and Healing
- Poor Self-Image
- Inhibitions
- Introversion
- PTSD
- And many more!

Are there any side-effects?

EFT rarely has any side effects. It is often combined with, or used instead of other procedures because of its gentle nature. People usually feel quite energised after an EFT session. Other side effects are advantageous ones, where treating one problem will cause another problem to heal almost spontaneously.

It is advisable to drink plenty of water after a session. If you already drink the normal daily recommended amount, this should suffice. It takes a lot to drink too much water!

How long do the results last?

If all underlying issues are resolved, then it is unlikely for symptoms to reappear. Results gained using EFT are almost always permanent. Physical healings can be impressive and enduring as well, but are more likely to re-emerge than emotional issues. Certain serious conditions may only receive temporary relief, yet there have been cases where even these kinds of problems have been permanently eradicated.

How long will it take to heal?

Unfortunately there are no hard and fast rules which can be applied here, because every condition and every person is different. Deeply rooted behaviours or beliefs will take longer to eliminate than some more simple problems. Usually a person with even the most deeply rooted problems will start seeing real benefits within (at worst) a few weeks, and some people (at best) within a few minutes. These techniques can rid us of the surplus emotional baggage, so we are free to get on with our lives and realise our full potential.

How do I find a good EFT Practitioner?

If you plan on visiting an E.F.T. Practitioner, I recommend looking for one with some sort of Psychotherapy skills too. Knowing about "cause and effect" will in my mind be an invaluable skill when it comes to getting rid of your symptoms in the quickest time possible. That said; an experienced practitioner will no doubt pick up similar insights by working with clients on a regular basis. Use your own judgement, do some research and check credentials before handing over your hard earned money. Things to look for:

- See if they belong to AAMET which is the main EFT Professional body.
- Check their certificate is genuine and not just a copy. An AAMET certificate will have a Golden Foil seal in the corner and an "ink" signature from the course instructor.
- Check they have a current public liability insurance certificate.
- See if they have any Testimonials from past clients.
- Ask if they can provide you with any personal case studies, which should not actually identify an individual.

Now I've said this, I best provide one!

Quick Case Study

I helped a client who was approached by someone covered in blood and brandishing a knife. Although, it turned out it was in fact his own blood, because he had been stabbed and was only seeking assistance; it still caused my client to think he was about to be stabbed and fear for his own life. This caused my client to struggle to sleep. When he did manage to sleep; he always awoke with the image of this blood soaked, knife wielding person in his mind.

After just one session of purely E.F.T., using one of the techniques I am going to share with you shortly; my client could replay the event in his mind quite calmly, and tell me about the incident without any emotion. Even after 12 months, he reported back he had not lost another night's sleep, was actually sleeping more soundly than before the incident occurred, and was exhibiting no symptoms whatsoever since our session.

Chapter 13

The "Basic Recipe"

They use some weird terminology in E.F.T.; one being the first Technique you learn is called a "recipe". I'm afraid I have no idea why, and to be honest; I'm not bothered, it's just semantics!

When you first see the technique, it looks really, really odd. For those old enough to remember "The Goodies"; I think you look a bit like you're doing the "Funky Gibbon" at one stage! Then there's something called "The 9 Gamut" which at first glance makes no sense at all. Once you have done Level 2 Training; you don't even use it again. I have included it in the video and this book because I am not training you to be a therapist; merely providing information.

The "Set Up Phrase"

To start off you will be tapping on the "Karate Chop" point (See picture on page 73) whilst repeating a phrase 3 times. This is called the "set up phrase":

"Even though I (state problem), I deeply and completely Love and Accept myself"

If you struggle with the ending you can delete the word "love" or change it to:

"Even though I (state problem), other than that I'm fine".

After this you repeat what the "problem" is (also known as the "reminder phrase") and tap on the other points in numerical order.

Example: "Even though I have agonising toothache, I deeply and completely love and accept myself" is repeated 3 times whilst tapping on the "Karate Chop" point. Then as you tap on each of the other points you say "agonising toothache".

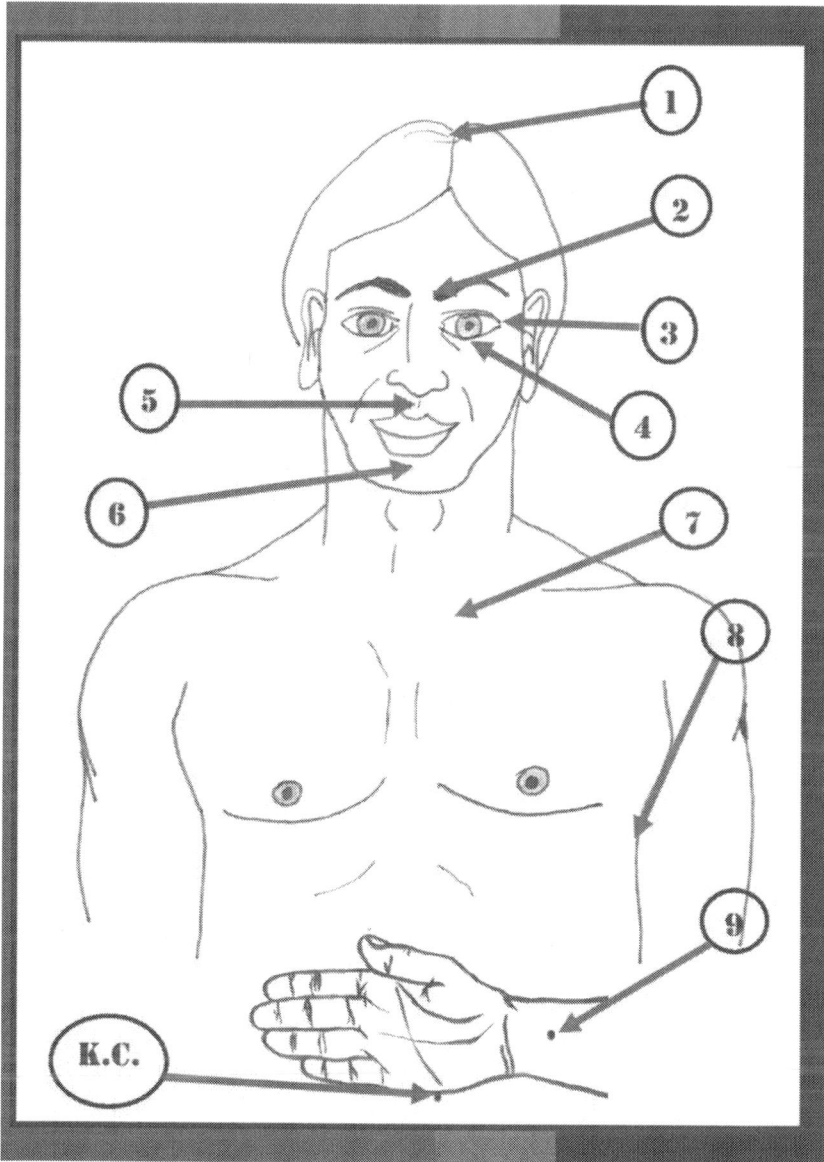

Image 7: The tapping points in numerical order, and the position of the "Karate Chop" point used during the "Set up Phrase".

EFT TAPPING POINTS

1. CROWN POINT
2. EYEBROW POINT
3. OUTER EYE POINT
4. UNDER EYE POINT
5. UNDER NOSE POINT
6. CHIN POINT
7. COLLAR BONE POINT
8. UNDER ARM POINT
9. INNER WRIST POINT
K.C. KARATE CHOP POINT

Image 8: List of names of the individual tapping points.

A Word on Tapping

Use your index and middle finger to tap on the points between 5 – 7 times each with a light pressure. You need to feel you are doing it, but you don't want to be inflicting pain on yourself or end up with a black eye!

In Your Own Words

It is extremely important that you use your own descriptive words for the pain/emotion you are feeling at the time you are tapping. If you are "fucking furious", this is what you use, rather than saying "I'm slightly miffed!" The more descriptive and specific you can be, the better and faster the results will be.

The "Suds Scale"

Before you begin a round of tapping, you first must identify how intense the pain/emotion is in the present moment. I won't bore you with the details of why it's called the "Suds Scale"; it's just another one of those odd things in E.F.T. Just gauge what you are feeling in the present moment on a scale of 0 to 10. 0 is no pain or negative emotion, whilst 10 is extreme pain or negative emotion: i.e. "fucking agony" or "shit scared!"

The "9 Gamut" Procedure

Apparently this technique has something to do with using both hemispheres of the brain, but we don't need to go into depth on why it works in this book. Just give it a go and see if you get some positive results. After the first round of tapping you can add in the routine which is on the next page, before doing another set of tapping on the points 1 – 9 whilst repeating the "reminder phrase".

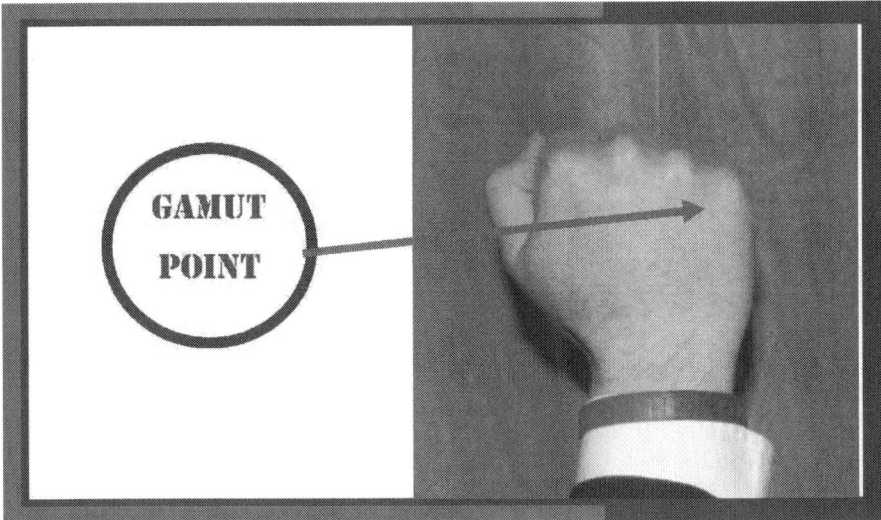

Image 9: The Gamut point is on the back of the hand between the little & ring finger, & about an inch towards the wrist.

Keep your head still, facing forward and Tap on the Gamut Point whilst you do the following:

- Stare straight ahead.
- Close your eyes (for a second or two)
- Open your eyes
- Look hard down to the left
- Look hard down to the right
- Roll your eyes in a circle clockwise
- Roll your eyes in a circle anti-clockwise
- Hum a simple unemotional tune for a few seconds (happy birthday is the standard)
- Count to 5 quickly
- Hum simple tune again for a few seconds.

Additional Rounds of Tapping

After the first round of tapping you will need to assess whether your pain/emotion has decreased or not using the "Suds Scale". Even if you use the "9 Gamut" and extra round of tapping; it is unlikely you will remove a symptom entirely in a single round if it scores above a 5.

In addition, the "Basic Recipe" is not the technique to use on its own to remove a memory associated with a traumatic event. Use it to work on a specific emotion or physical pain which you are experiencing in a particular moment.

Note: E.F.T. does not remove positive emotions such as Love, Joy, Happiness, etc. before you ask!

If Symptoms Are Reducing But Not Gone

You may have to do 3 or 4 rounds of tapping to get rid of each specific pain/emotion. In the second and subsequent rounds, all you need to do is alter the "set up phrase" slightly as in these Examples:

1. "Even though I have this remaining (problem), I deeply & ..."
2. "Even though I am still slightly (problem), I deeply & ..."
3. "Even though I have this last bit of (problem), other than that..."

Note on Pain

This is the nervous systems way of letting you know that something is not as it should be somewhere in your body. Therefore E.F.T. will not get rid of ALL the physical pain if there is actually a mechanical injury; but it will reduce the pain. Here is a Personal Example:

In 2009 whilst awaiting a date for surgery for a hernia operation I attended a party. After a few hours I succumbed to an urge to have 5 minutes on the adult Bouncy Castle; drinking Black Sambuca may have had something to do with it!

The result was I folded myself in half, popping 2 ribs off the sternum and causing soft tissue damage to my upper spine during the process. EFT never got the pain below a Suds Scale of 2; because the discomfort was a reminder of the fact I was not at optimal physical condition and could have caused more damage if I didn't rest. It also reminded me how stupid I'd been; Matelots eh?!!

Chapter 14

The "Movie Technique"

I will now share with you one of the more advanced techniques, but I would recommend either training to be an E.F.T. Practitioner or visiting one to do this properly. The main reason I say this is because when you work with deep rooted problems you may encounter "Unconscious Resistance", and in E.F.T. something called "Secondary Benefit Syndrome." You don't need to understand these concepts to use the technique, and as I have mentioned earlier in this book; I am providing information only. If you decide to try this technique of "Your Own Free Will" because you can't afford to train in E.F.T. or visit a therapist, you will most likely find it does reduce the severity of your P.T.S.D. symptoms. As in most things in life; there are no guarantees.

Side Note (Tangent): Do you agree with me, it is a sad state of affairs when you have to "cover your ass" when all you are trying to do is help people? First aiders getting sued for cracking ribs administering CPR to SAVE a life, Doctors afraid to use new techniques on terminally ill patients in case they kill them, and teachers not allowed to comfort an upset child because it could be interpreted as paedophilia; what a strange world we live in?! Sorry about the tangent there, but I am renown for them; ask any of my old clients. I'm sure they'll be another few before the end of this book!

Give it a Title

If you are having flashbacks and nightmares then you will have a mini-movie which is being played over and over in your mind about the traumatic event. This movie probably lasts a couple of minutes. So you need to give it a title as if it was a real movie. Once again you need to use your own words.

Personal Example: This example is just as it appeared in my original PDF version. I have left it virtually unchanged - only improving the grammar in places - because it captured an unexpected effect as I was writing it.

When I was in the Royal Navy, a shipmate fell off a car park roof whilst we were on a run ashore. The sound of him hitting the concrete still sends shivers down my spine to this day when I think about it. Obviously this was a traumatic event for the three of us who were with him. To the best of my knowledge, we all came to terms with this event over time. However, if the nightmares still persisted today, I would use this technique and the title of my movie would be "Fall of the Drunken Sailor".

First Round of Tapping

Once you have your "Movie Title", you need to do a round of tapping just the same as in the "Basic Recipe". There is no need to do the "9 Gamut" with this method.

My Example: I would have said "Even though I have this "Fall of the Drunken Sailor" Movie, I deeply and completely accept myself " three times whilst tapping on the "Karate Chop" point.
Then I would say "this 'Fall of the Drunken Sailor' Movie" as I tapped on the other nine points in numerical order.

Tell the Story

Difficult to do this on your own, but imagine you are telling the story of the "movie" event to someone else. You tell the story from the beginning until you feel some negative emotion appear. As soon as you feel this emotion, you stop the story there and tap on whatever the emotion is. This could take a few rounds of tapping to completely get rid of it.

My Example: "He was mucking about hanging off the edge of the car park, suddenly he disappeared from sight and I realised he had fallen."

In the present moment, I feel "numb (even now as I recall it) and I want to cry". On the "Suds Scale", this is a 7.

(I wasn't actually expecting to be doing this for real when I started typing. I have just shed a small tear, and will in reality do a round of tapping now.)

First round of tapping over and it is now a "3" on the "Suds Scale".

Now I start another round of tapping: "Even though I still feel a little numb and want to cry, I deeply and completely love and accept myself" is repeated 3 times as I tap on the "Karate Chop" point. Then "still feel a little numb and want to cry" is said as I tap on each of the other tapping points in numerical order. Second round of tapping completed and the numbness has disappeared; and I no longer feel the urge to cry.

Note: This just goes to show, even though we think we have come to terms with an event, it is not always the case. I genuinely wasn't expecting to exhibit any strong emotions in using my example.

Continue with the Story

Once you have reduced the emotion to a "zero" on the "Suds Scale", you start telling the story again from the beginning until you encounter another emotion. Then you stop and work on this emotion until it has gone. You keep doing this until you can tell the whole "movie" calmly and without any negative emotions.

My Example: "He was mucking about hanging off the edge of the car park, suddenly he disappeared from sight and I realised he had fallen. There was absolute silence from all of us, which seemed to last an eternity; it was almost surreal. Then the silence was broken by…"

I will not finish this sentence, but needless to say this is where I am feeling some level of emotion and need to do some work on myself at some future point.

Lost Shipmate

Although I did not include what follows in the original PDF, I thought this book would make more sense if I added a bit more of what happened in my example.

After we rushed down the stairs and found our friend lying in a puddle of his blood, and making a gurgling sound; the police arrived and did little. We made sure his airway was clear as we waited for the ambulance to arrive. We accompanied him to the hospital and stayed as long as we could before we had to return to the ship, which was due to sail for a weekend exercise.

The Sailors Mess on a Type 22 Frigate is home to about 54 Matelots, and the mood was extremely solemn as we spent a very long few days at sea. After the ship returned and the work day finished, a few of us returned to the hospital, to find our friends parents sitting anxiously. They had a terrible decision to make in the next few days; but they allowed us to say our goodbyes first.

We then went out on the piss, to drown our sorrows and toast farewell to a good shipmate. This was the closest thing to grief counselling we would get.

We did the same thing in Newcastle after the funeral; we went on a "rig run", because this was the only coping mechanism we knew. The military machine expects you to just get back on with things, and we did with a little help from our oppos. I just hope there is better aftercare nowadays for those who lose a fallen comrade. Now back to the EFT...

Unexpected Change In Emotion

You may be tapping away on an emotion with a "Suds Scale" of 4, when you suddenly feel a new and stronger emotion appear. If this should happen, you work on the new emotion instead until it is reduced to a "Zero" on the "Suds Scale".

Note: This can also happen with physical ailments and is known as "chasing the pain". You could be working on a shoulder pain, and then the pain moves to your neck. If this happens (and often does), it is nothing to worry about; just work on the new pain.

Chapter 15

The "Tree Metaphor"

You do not need to know all about the "Tree Metaphor" used in E.F.T., but just as in the video I will briefly share my personal take on it.

The tree can be broken down into 3 main areas (see image 10):

1) Main "General" Problem
2) Aspects of the Problem
3) Unconscious Elements of the Problem

If we tap on just the main "general" problem, we are very unlikely to find total resolution. There will always be "aspects" to the problem, and quite often some "unconscious elements" which will pop up. These are the parts of the "tree" we work on with our tapping.

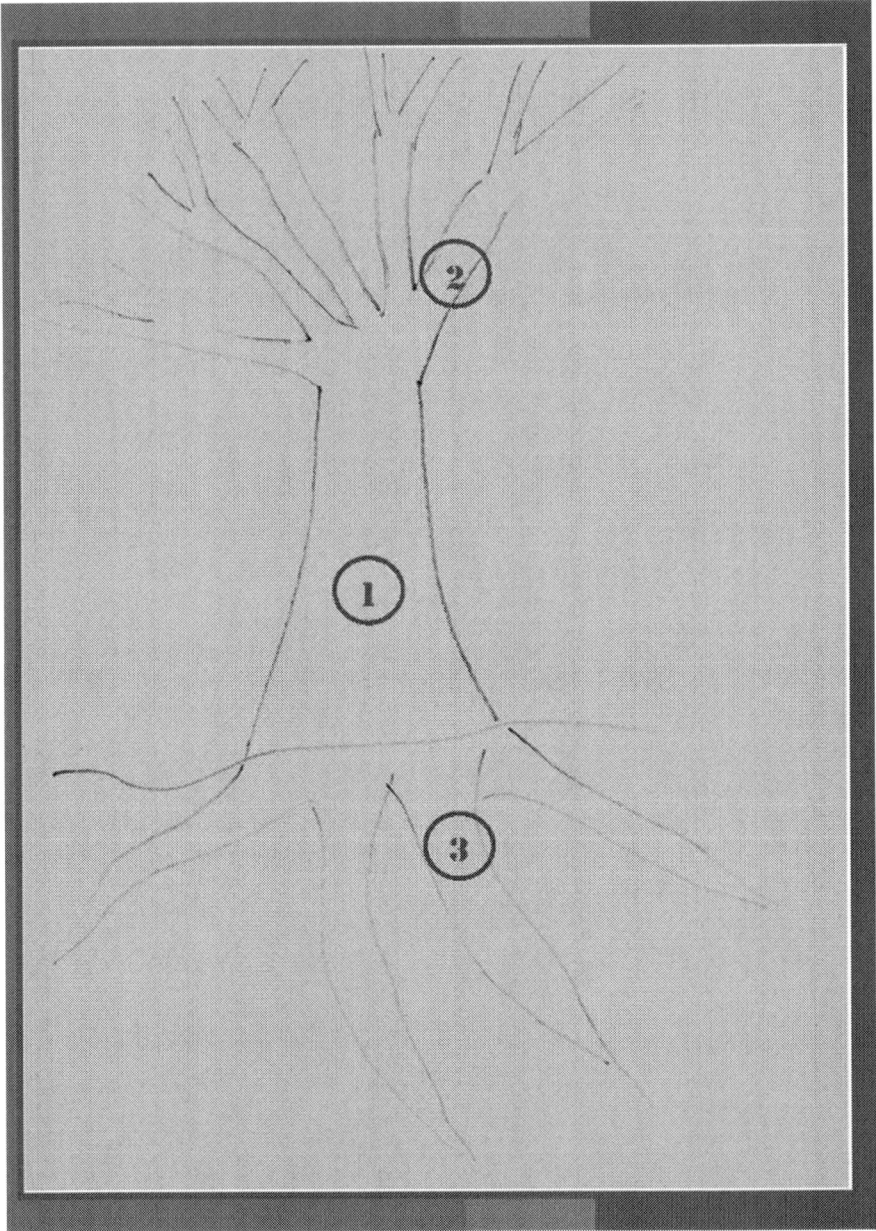

Image 10: The Tree Metaphor

Felling the Tree

When we tap on individual aspects of a problem (and unconscious elements when they appear) we metaphorically take the tree apart piece by piece. We do not need to work on every aspect or element to fell the tree.

Most human beings don't have just one solitary tree causing them concern in their lives; but rather something resembling a small grove to a vast forest!

Another advantage E.F.T. can provide is when you chop down one tree; it can knock down another couple with it. I.E. you don't need to work on every single one of your horde of problems to become a well-rounded, emotionally stable, psychologically integrated Homo sapiens.

Side Note (Tangent): How weird, Microsoft Word did not offer any suggestions when I incorrectly spelt Homo sapiens as "Homosapiens"?!!

Tree Metaphor Example: Fear of Flying

With the multitude of phobias I could have used as an example, I find it almost ironic to have picked aerophobia; because to complete this book I will have launched myself out of an aeroplane!

1. If we just tap on "fear of flying" which is the "main trunk" of the problem, it is very unlikely to disappear.
2. Instead we tap on the individual "aspect branches" one at a time until they cause us no more negative emotion.

For our example these could be:

- A feeling of being trapped.
- A feeling of being out of control.
- Worry a wing will fall off the plane.
- Concern there may be a terrorist on board.
- The pilot might become sick, etc.

3. Whilst we are working on an aspect, an unexpected "root" cause may surface. We will not know where it came from and usually may not be certain whether the memory associated with the emotion is real or not. Removing the "root problem" of a tree will fell it far quicker than working on the aspects. So if unsure; tap on it if there is any emotion.

For our example this could be:

- A childhood memory of being locked in a cupboard.
- A vivid memory of what you were doing when you first heard about 9/11.
- Or a multitude of what may seem like unrelated causes.

Chapter 16

My Skydive For Combat Stress

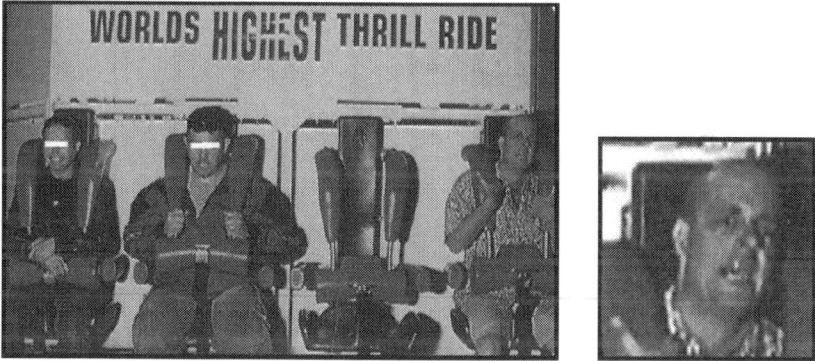

Image 11 & 12: The Look Of Terror & A Close Up!

History of Fear

In November 2000 I went to visit an Ex-Navy oppo - who was my best man – in Berkeley, California. Because he was working during the week, I hired a car and drove to Las Vegas for 24 hours. These pictures were taken when I went on that silly ride on top of "The Stratosphere". I share these pictures to show, and prove how much I hate heights. Yes, I convinced myself to go on it, but as you can see; I didn't exactly enjoy it. Unlike the lady on the left of the picture, who clearly was and puts me to shame; she looks like she's just relaxing in her favourite armchair!

It Worked!

In the introduction to this book I said I would share my experience of a Tandem Skydive, and how I would use EFT to get me to be able to do it. I'm pleased to say, it worked and what an amazing experience it was. If you've ever considered doing one, I highly recommend it.

I'm not a natural worrier, and I tend to take each moment as it comes. However, with something as scary as jumping out of a perfectly good aeroplane, I did begin to worry in the week building up to the event. On the day, I even left a list of all my passwords with my laptop, so this book would still get published if it all went wrong! But, because I said in the introduction I would not do any work on my fear until the day, I resisted the extremely strong temptation to do so. At approx. 0001Hrs on 11th June 2011, I began some tapping!

What follows is a list of the feelings and thoughts I tapped on in no particular order, including the original level on the "Scuds Scale", before I managed to get 4 hours sleep. Some are daft as you will see, but I've included them to show how ridiculous the mind can be when it comes to fear:

- Scared about doing skydive (6)
- Afraid I'm going to die (6)
- Afraid I'm going to be afraid during the skydive (7)
- Afraid I'm going to shit myself literally (5)

- Scared I'll panic during free-fall (6)
- Afraid I'll fall out of the harness (8)
- Scared I'll panic in the plane (4)
- Afraid I'll die having achieved nothing with my life (3)
- Afraid I'll never get laid again! (3)

As you see some of these fears weren't really related to my fear of heights, but just popped up. Essentially I used the "basic recipe" on all these weird and wonderful thoughts until they were either gone, or at least severely reduced. The first round of tapping was done on the general "trunk" of the fear, i.e. "scared of doing a skydive". Then I worked on the aspects or "branches" of the fear, which is the rest of the list.

I awoke calm and refreshed at 0530hrs, which is usually associated with bedtime, not getting up for me. After walking the dog I did a round of tapping on "even though I'm still slightly nervous" and then awaited the arrival of my chauffeur, my Mum.

On the two hour drive to the Duke of Gloucester Barracks, I listened to a 20 minute meditation on my iPod, and did one round of tapping on "these remaining nerves".

We arrived in good time and I felt exceptionally calm during the briefing. After a quick visit to the heads – which I noticed seem to take some hammer – it was time to get the kit on and take off.

The small plane was packed and I remained calm as we climbed to around 3000 feet, when the door opened and a static line jumper bailed out, and the door was closed again. The guy I was attached to was giving me instructions which I could barely hear as we climbed to 12000 feet. I was thinking to myself "this is fucking it, no turning back now" and felt a little apprehensive at this stage, and just did a little tapping on the "karate chop" point.

I started using motivational images to calm down my trepidation of what was imminent, such as the scene from "Star Wars Episode II – Attack of the Clones", when Anakin jumps out of the speeder over Coruscant; yes, I know very Geeky!

When the door opened again, the remaining jumpers took it in turns to bail out, leaving just me, my instructor – Paul, and the cameraman - Ben. Oh, and of course, the pilot.

Here was my moment with destiny, but there was a problem with the camera, and so we had to circle the airfield a couple of times whilst he tried to fix it. I started thinking to myself "fuck the camera; let's get on with it, before I change my mind!" Even though I had this thought, I was still extremely calm given the circumstances. Ben said we'd have to do without any "still" pictures, and so we got ready to go.

Ben climbed out on to the side of the plane first, whilst I was given my final instructions, as we shuffled to the doorway and assumed the position. I can't be sure whether I initially closed my eyes for the briefest of seconds as we exited or not. What I do remember, was shouting "this is fucking awesome" as we reached terminal velocity. It was a weird feeling, it didn't seem like you were falling, just the wind and moisture from the clouds whizzing past you. I have to give full credit to Ben, who managed to take "still" pictures manually whilst descending at 120 mph.

It didn't seem longer than a few seconds before the chute deployed and our descent slowed down. I still had the tiniest bit of fear remaining, yet nothing compared to what I had felt when I tried parascending in Mexico back in 1995; which I didn't enjoy. As I chatted to Paul, I was allowed to take control briefly and when asked if I fancied a faster descent, I replied, "yeah, why not!"

I was expecting to want to kiss the ground when we landed, yet my thoughts when we did were "I want to do that again". I had no shakes, my legs had not turned to jelly, and I was actually smiling. Prior to this, I'd rather have been on the upper scupper in a sea state 10, than even contemplate partaking in skydiving. Yet as I write this; I am considering a static line jump next!

So there you have it, I am living proof of the effectiveness of the techniques outlined in this section of the book. Many of us therapists are hypocrites in the sense we proffer "do as I say, not as I do" advice. I for one have helped hundreds of people to quit smoking, and yet smoke myself, although now I have landed safely I am intending to quit. There was no point quitting before the jump was my rationale for continuing.

Side Note (Tangent): No idea why the word "proffer" just popped into my mind as I was typing, not a word I recall ever using before; weird, but I like it!

This concludes my brief guide to E.F.T. It is by no means comprehensive, but I hope it will benefit you in some way. If you want to learn more about the subject, then I highly recommend training in this discipline, you will not regret it, and unlike psychotherapy; it doesn't cost too much or take long to train either.

Image 13: After the Jump with Camera Man - Sgt Ben Cannon, & Instructor - Paul Kendall from Silver Stars R.L.C. Parachute Centre. Thanks Guys.

You can watch the video of my first skydive at this link: www.youtube.com/user/skilledexforces

Section 4: Bonus Tips

The following 10 tips on increasing your general wellbeing are a short introduction to another book I am planning on writing; which if written will go into greater depth and detail. At the time of writing, I only have the rough outline of what I intend to cover. So I am sharing a little of what is to come, because I think they are just as relevant to sufferers of PTSD, and are still very useful in their current concise description.

There is a hidden undercurrent running through most, maybe all of them; so see if you can spot what it is. This will definitely be beneficial to anyone who suffers any form of anxiety. One hint, if you think it is the notion it seems a bit "far out" or "new age", you will be wrong; even if these particular statements may have a grain of truth to them!

I have to admit, if someone was to tell me I would write something like what is about to follow when I was still in the mob; I would have thought they were insane, even if I have always been into weird shit. Although in this case; the weird shit which I'm about to present to you is well researched, and only really scratches the surface of each tip.

Side Note (Tangent): Why do they call it "New Age", when most of what fits in this category is from ancient teachings?

Chapter 17

Control What Your Senses Experience

Our experience of life is governed by our five main senses. Although they do not give a true depiction of how the world or even the Universe really is; they are still the best and only bit of kit we have for understanding the myriad of stimuli we encounter on a daily basis.

The main sense most of us use to discern reality is our sight, followed by hearing; whilst the others we seldom pay too much close conscious attention to. There are many techniques for becoming more consciously aware with all our senses, more of the time, and we'll cover a brief introduction to the subject in this chapter. For now we're just going to look at how we can use our senses to improve our overall wellbeing quickly. My suggestion is to pick just one sense to work with for an entire day and fully explore it as much as humanly possible, without looking too weird to other people.

Smell

Let's face it, compared to a dog, we can smell sweet F.A., but even still it is a sense which can be developed, heightened and used to calm the tensions in our bodies. Incense and aromatherapy oils may be the first thing which springs to mind after my previous sentence; and this is a pretty good place to start. If you use the right scent, at the right time in your home; they can help you to overcome all manner of ills. However, if you consider yourself to be too macho to go into one of those hippy shops; I have an alternative. Simply spend the entire day noticing all the natural fragrances you encounter as you go about your normal business. Some, you will enjoy, some you won't, and others you may wonder what they are exactly. It may not be a good idea to explore the variety of odours found in the mess!

Taste

Although apparently we cannot taste anything if we can't smell it first, we can still dedicate a day to stimulate this sense. Purposely trying new flavours for a full day will be more rewarding than you may think; and the effect it will have on your general wellbeing needs to be experienced, not explained. This is not an excuse to have a pig-out on your favourite comfort food!

Touch

If your mind has already entered the gutter; please drag it back out for a moment. As you go about you daily activities, you can do this exercise with just your hands, exploring the sensations which we just normally take for granted. Exploring diverse textures with different areas of the body will get you focused entirely in the present, and it will make you feel more alive. If you have a partner, you can also do this with each other. OK, now you can return your mind back to the gutter!

Hearing

Listening to soothing music is an obvious activity for the days you dedicate to your sense of hearing. However, I would also suggest you pay close attention to other sounds in your environment; especially if you can get out into nature.

Playing motivational or educational programs are a great distraction, and the bonus is you are increasing your knowledge base at the same time. I have found I am much more motivated, cheerful and achieve so much more in my day; even if they are only playing in the background.

Sight

This is most people's primary sense; and this is why I have left it until last. The good old saying; "A picture says a thousand words" is really a bit of an understatement. A visual experience, even a simple picture can affect our emotional state instantly; more than almost any other stimulus. If you look at the following picture, you will more than likely experience some level of negative emotion.

Image 14: Damn scary looking spider.

From "eew" to "aghh!" the people who would find this picture anything other, are in the minority. The vast majority of spiders pose no real threat to us though, yet they make the "Top Ten List" of human fears. It seems to be an inherited primal fear, and so maybe some serious big ass spiders used to terrorise our ancestors, maybe not!

As you look at this picture, which causes you the most discomfort:

- Is it those eight emotionless beady little eyes staring at you?
- Is it those nasty looking fangs awaiting the next meal?
- Or is it something totally different going on in your own imagination?

Image 15: Sleeping puppies, how cute.

In contrast, when you look at this picture, I hope it creates a warm & pleasant feeling within you. There has got to be something inhuman about anyone who does not go all gooey and soft inside when they look at this picture. Although many people are afraid of dogs, I am yet to meet someone who is terrified of puppies; although I'm certain they exist.

I could have quite easily used pictures which would have provoked a stronger emotional response, and no doubt will if I turn these bonus tips into a book in their own right, but I didn't think the images I have in mind would be suitable in a book on PTSD. Instead, the fact you have served in the Military, suggests to me, you are a switched on cookie, and will understand the concept I'm putting across without the need for more graphic images.

If a mere black and white picture in a book can affect your emotions so easily, it only makes logical sense to fill your field of vision with images of beauty, humour and even love as much as you can. We shall explore how in the next chapter.

Chapter 18

TV/Media

Image 16: You know you've been there guys!

When we watch movies and TV we become affected by what we see if the content is especially emotive. A good thriller will have the hairs standing up on the back of your neck; just as if some psycho was really stalking you. And I don't care how macho you think you are; I know you, like me, have watched some "chick flick" and found the "room to get a little smoky"!

But why do we exhibit such emotions? After all, we know it isn't real; it's just some actors playing a part. As mentioned earlier in this book; our nervous system cannot tell the difference between a real event, and a vividly imagined one. So as we view these works of fiction, we become passive bystanders drawn into the reality of whoever is responsible for the content of the show or movie. The same is true of real life events which we encounter in the media, be it TV, tabloid, or even the internet. Knowing this, you can now begin to limit the amount of negative stimulus you allow into your field of vision.

I personally have never purchased a newspaper on a regular basis, and I can't even remember the last time I bought one. It certainly wasn't this decade, century or even millennium. I even got rid of my TV licence in 2010 because I had got to the point where I was forcing myself to watch TV just to justify the cost. I have set up my web browsers homepage to not have any news headlines appearing when I open it. What's your point, you're probably thinking right now, yes? The point is, even without these usual sources of keeping track of world events, I still manage to know what is going on in the world; well most of the time anyway. I can assure you my life is not adversely affected if I do happen to miss some titbit of celebrity gossip, a major catastrophe, or even some sporting achievement. For any particular subject which interests me, I simply search the internet for related articles to keep abreast of the current situation, and do not overload myself with any of its negative aspects. I still watch movies, quite a lot actually, but these are ones I choose to watch, when I want to watch them, not just because they are on at the time.

I read somewhere, our happiness levels drop by something like 5% for every hour of TV we watch. So if you are suffering from PTSD, I advise you to avoid the soap operas, most reality shows, and the News if you can. As I said, you will still know what is going on in the world and let's face it; knowing about it, won't change it.

At the start of this book, I prescribed you a daily dose of laughter, so watching a good comedy often should be more than enough to satisfy your media fix, if you feel you cannot survive without TV.

Chapter 19

Change Your Posture, Move Your Body, And Smile

Posture

Believe it or not, how you sit or stand affects your mood. The following series of pictures will clarify what I'm talking about.

Image 17: How not to sit when you aren't feeling too pipper!

Even if you are feeling absolutely amazing when you first adopt the posture in Image 17, after staying in it for too long; you will notice an adverse effect on your mood. So avoid assuming this pose at all costs. We were told to sit up straight when we were children. Yet little did we realise at the time, what great advice this was. Not only is it good for maintaining a healthy normal curvature of the spine; but also beneficial for general wellbeing.

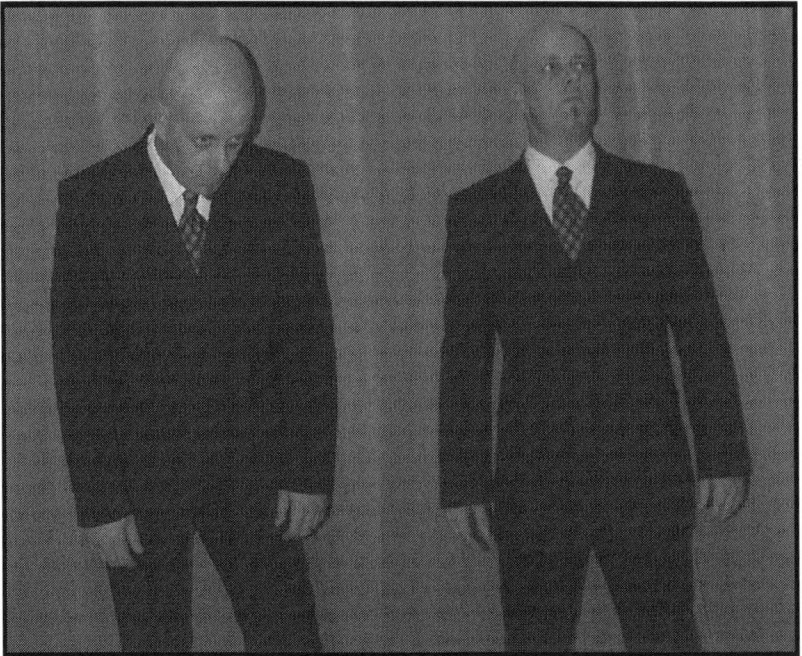

Image 18: No, it's not the Mitchell Brothers!

The stance on the left is not quite as detrimental as the previous one, but it will still make you feel lethargic and is often assumed by those with low self-esteem or lacking confidence; and teenagers of course!

Try assuming this pose now and notice how you feel, then immediately adopt the one from the right of the picture.
Did you notice a difference?
If not, and if no one is watching try alternating between the two poses, spending around 20 seconds in each. Do this several times and pay close attention. You will notice a significant difference in how you feel if you keep at it.

If someone was watching you unbeknownst, and ask you what you were doing. I have an excuse for you: tell them you were doing a Meer cat impression.
Sorry, maybe not the best excuse in the world, however I'm going a little silly at the end of this page, to prepare you for the one which follows next!

Image 19: Hallelujah, now give me your money!

I have already mentioned earlier in this book how it is impossible to be in two conflicting emotional states. This is true with your posture too. By adopting an upright and confident position, it is nigh on impossible to feel miserable or depressed. The problem comes with maintaining this sort of bearing for long, because it requires conscious effort. As soon as we become distracted by something in our environment, or by our own thoughts, we slip back into the old negative stance.

If you are feeling low, and assuming one of the negative poses from the previous pictures then try this: reach up to, and face the ceiling, and then begin to pull silly faces. Keep at it for a few minutes and you will soon find your mood elevating. If I can do it in a picture available for the whole world to see just for your benefit; then I'm sure you can give it a go in the privacy of your own home!

I wish I could credit the person who I learnt this idea from, but unfortunately it is something I came across over 10 years ago. However, the important thing is, it works, so go do it now, go on!

Exercise

I'm sure you already know regular exercise is proven to be good for you. We release endorphins which make us feel happy, so I won't dwell on the science any more than this. Remembering this fact though, is another matter when you are not at your best. If you are feeling in a low mood, you may not feel the urge to do something strenuous; so a mere 10 minute walk round the block may be all you need to lift your spirits, and maybe this will even motivate you to do some more.

If getting out of the house is a no-no because of the weather, firstly don't be such a wussy! Only joking, it takes a lot to get motivated to go for a walk when it's hammering it down; even if you've got a dog crossing its legs and staring at you impatiently. So if you are housebound for whatever reason and need to elevate your spirits, how about putting on some tunes and cutting a mean rug?

Image 20: Move over John T., Disco Stu is in the House!

Shake your wicked hoof for a few minutes and you'll soon be feeling better. The great thing is, you may not be some disco king (or queen) and only be able of performing the Matelot shuffle, but no one is going to see you; so there is no need to be self-conscious. My bezzie oppo and I were always first on the dance floor on runs ashore, even if there was no one else on it. I've even danced 6 miles home from a party because the tunes on my iPod happened to be really banging. Needless to say, I was incredibly drunk at the time!

Personally, I'd definitely say dancing is my second favourite form of exercise. I'm sure it's hardly worth mentioning as I'm certain you know this already, but my first favourite type of exercise is an incredible remedy for the blues too.

Extra Bonus Tip: If your partner ever uses the excuse "I have a headache", you can point out it has been proven scientifically, one of the best cures for a headache is an orgasm!

Smile

At the start of this book I prescribed you to take at least a daily dose of laughter. I've also mentioned a few times about not being able to be in two conflicting emotional states.

Side Note (Tangent): You find this happens quite a lot in reference books and factual documentaries. I think in part it is just to make the damn thing longer. Especially in those "hidden secrets" type of documentaries where you often hear, "after the break you'll find out how so and so managed to keep such and such hidden from another so and so for nearly fifty years!" Then after the break they go through nearly everything which happened in the previous thirty minutes, before the often disappointing secret is finally revealed at the very end of the show. However, in self-help types of books we do it, to hammer the point home!

Image 21: Well I did say I'd include some "Pretty Pictures"!

Ok, back to smiling. When you smile, you feel good and this once again is scientifically proven in case it wasn't obvious. Nevertheless, people just don't seem to do it as often as they could. If you begin to start smiling to everyone you pass during your day, you will usually find a curious thing will happen; the other person will smile back. The result of this is; you both feel slightly better than you did moments before. One caveat, don't do this when you're out on the piss; unless you want to get into a ruck!

As an experiment, I once spent a whole day walking my dog and smiling at everyone I encountered; and I'd say about 95% of people did indeed smile back. I took the dog with me so as not to appear mad or intimidating, because unfortunately we have become so paranoid in the western world, we think there is a terrorist, a paedophile or other type of criminal waiting around every corner, ready to pounce and do us over. Whilst it is true, these people do exist; fortunately they are in the minority.

If more of us made an effort to be a little friendlier, I'm certain we could soon counter this mistrustful meme which has become so prevalent. I mean, have you ever travelled on the London underground? I had to abandon my experiment when I tried it there because people on this form of transport can't even make eye contact, never mind smile!

Chapter 20:

Do Something Different

Image 22: New hobby? Maybe not!

A great way to inject a bit of a buzz into your life is to take up a new hobby. Although mastering a new skill can be a little frustrating at first; the sense of accomplishment cannot be beaten when you see you are beginning to become proficient at it. If this new hobby involves getting out of the house and joining a group, even better, because you will meet other people and probably make some new friends.

You will also be forming new neural pathways in your brain, which I assure you in this way, is a good thing. We can also do this by changing a behavioural pattern too.

As creatures of habit, these behaviours often become so ingrained, we have no conscious clue how we do them. Let me demonstrate. I want you to answer the following question immediately:

Which sock do you put on first, left or right?

Even as I typed the question out, I couldn't even answer it with any certainty, how about you? Are you about to take your socks off, and then put them back on to find out? I did, and discovered I felt inclined to put the left one on first!

Although it is good to have these stored patterns which make life easier, we can still play about with them a bit to form a new neural pathway, and at the same time, increase our already vast skillset. For the minimum of a few days, work on one of your normal daily habits in a completely different way. It may take a focused conscious effort to do it, but it can be fun.

Here are a few more examples to get you started:

- Use your non-dominant hand to write any "notes to self".
- If you normally turn left out the door when walking the dog, turn right instead and see where your feet take you.
- Rearrange the order of your morning routine.

Our minds do a good job of protecting us by keeping things familiar and regular as much as possible. However it does you good to get out of your comfort zone every now and again; this is how we learn and grow. Change is a constant in the Universe, and the contrary is just an illusion.

Forming a new behaviour so it becomes unconscious takes between 21 – 28 days, but once it's in the unconscious, it becomes a part of you and very difficult to get rid of. This is why smokers struggle to quit; other than normal bodily functions such as breathing; there is nothing a person does so often on a daily basis. If the "habit" of smoking isn't dealt with correctly, then a person can get back into it years later. It usually starts with a couple of draws on someone else's cigarette, then borrowing the odd one, before finally succumbing to buying your own and then the old behavioural pattern kicks back in in full swing.

Side Note (Tangent): I did want to actually write "you start off by bumming a fag", but if this book is read by an American, they might get the wrong idea!

Any repeated action can become second nature to you with a little persistence. I found it interesting during my research to find a report which suggests it takes the average learner driver 21 lessons to pass their test. If you remember your first driving lesson, I'm sure you like me, thought "I'll never get the hang of all these different things I need to do at the same time". Yet, now if you were to explain the process of driving to a total novice, it would take a concerted conscious effort to do so, because unless something untoward happens when we are driving, or we are in unfamiliar territory; our minds are usually somewhere else, and not where they really should be. Saying this though, those of us who ride bikes, and drive, tend to be more attentive to road conditions than those who only drive. Yes, our weaving through the traffic like a bat out of hell may seem inconsiderate and dangerous, but you can only do this if you are entirely focused in the moment. This doesn't make us immune to being away with the fairies occasionally, just not as often.

When we become an experienced driver, it's almost like we have consciously forgotten how to drive, and do it by instinct. Look at other areas of your life where you work in this way, and see if there is a way to do it differently, or practice a new skill until it works in this manner; both will be beneficial to you.

Chapter 21

Question Yourself

Image 23: Not the "Blue Man Group" on a day off either!

A really powerful way to improve your general wellbeing and expand your view of the world is to regularly question yourself. Just like in the saying from the N.L.P. section "the map is not the territory", many of our beliefs and assumptions are incorrect. If we make a conscious effort to question these opinions, we will become a much more psychologically integrated individual.

A belief put simply is a piece of information which we have a strong emotional attachment to, or take for granted. Yet many of these ideas do not stand up to close scrutiny. For example, someone might say "No one ever does anything for me." Is this really true? So who made the clothes they are wearing? Who was it who taught them to read? Who is showing them the courtesy of listening to their complaint?

Many people believe "all wars are caused by religion", yet they are just a banner to hide behind to motivate people to fight to protect something they consider sacred to them; whilst in reality most wars in human history have been caused by the greed of a few people in positions of power.

So in some ways it could be said, beliefs take away our freedom to choose for ourselves, hold us back from realising our full potential, and restrict us to a relatively mundane existence. If instead, we just hold opinions which are open to change when new data appears to contradict our previous assumptions, we will be less likely to become emotionally unstable when a personal view is challenged. We do this quite easily as we move through our childhood with such beliefs as Santa or the Tooth Fairy, yet find it difficult to do in adulthood.

Here are a few sample questions to ask yourself about absolutely any belief you hold:

- How long have you had it?
- Where did you first get it from?
- How reliable is it?

Let's use a simple example of a common false belief and see how it holds up to these three questions: Marconi invented radio.

1. If you believe this - as I used to - you've probably had the belief since childhood.
2. You would have got this idea from school, TV, or your parents, etc.
3. In 1943, The Supreme Court in the U.S. ruled that Marconi had essentially stolen the patents of Nikola Tesla to develop his radio equipment. This happened 28 years before I was born, so how did I end up being provided with this unreliable belief?

I chose this example, because it is provable, and unlikely to cause anyone to get overly emotional. Marconi obviously has his part to play in the development of radio, but cannot be credited as the inventor; neither can Tesla for that matter. Though I'm going a little off topic; if you are interested in the invention of radio, look up James Clerk Maxwell and Heinrich Hertz; they had a part to play too. Despite being the genius he was, many people have never even heard of Nikola Tesla; nor had I until I was in my late twenties. So if the truth behind something so common place, and taken for granted like utilising radio waves can be such a common misconception; what others beliefs do you have which are false?

After you have quizzed yourself in this way about some of your personal beliefs, you may want to try this exercise to really expand your consciousness:

For a day, assume the exact opposite, or at least an alternative of what you currently believe. After all, there will be a great number of people on the planet who think this way every day of their lives. This enlightening exercise will reduce your desire to prejudge people for the way they look, their religious or political inclinations, or sexual preferences, etc. For example, if you believe promiscuity is a sin – although unlikely if you've served – then for a day, you can imagine how you'd think and behave if you thought it was the only way of life!

By the way, have you picked up on the hidden undercurrent in these tips yet?

Chapter 22

Do Something For Someone Else

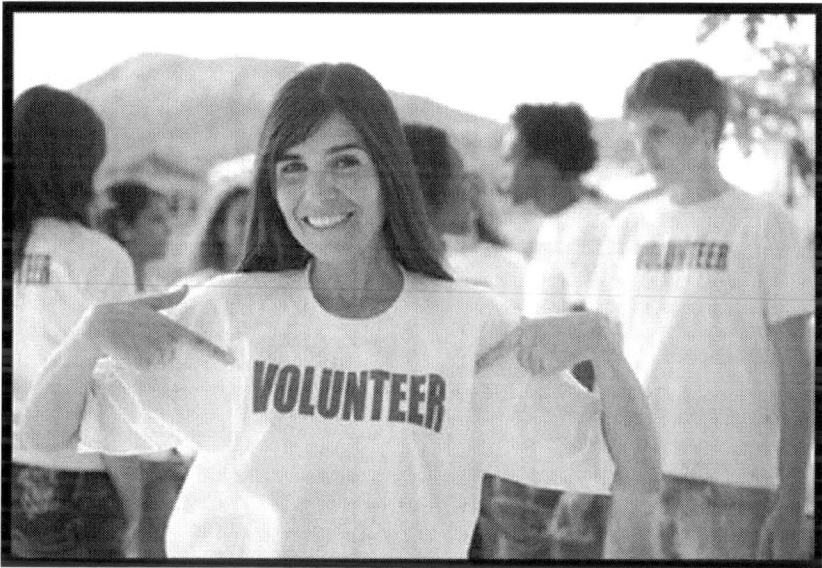

Image 24: Is it just me who thinks she's pointing at something other than the word "Volunteer"? My Bad!

Ever notice how one of the greatest feelings of joy you have experienced doesn't involve self-gratification? Maybe you haven't exactly noticed it, but I'd wager it's true. If you have children - which as far as I'm aware, I don't - isn't the highlight of your Christmas watching their faces as they open their presents? I'm told this is the case anyway. However, even if like me, you haven't got kids, you will no doubt still know the joy of giving a gift to someone you hold dear. So why limit this feeling to birthdays and religious holidays, when you can experience it daily. There are so many ways in which you can do something for someone else, I suppose I could write a book devoted to just this subject; but not today.

But to get the old cogs turning a bit, here's a few suggestions to get you started:

1. Genuinely listen to someone else's problem: Doing this can take the edge off your own problems when you realise other people have things bad too. If you can go on to alleviate their concerns in any way, you will get an extra buzz of self-worth.

2. Tell a story to cheer them up: at the time it can feel as if we have things worse than anyone else on the planet. Although this is unlikely to be true, sharing a tale to cheer someone up can be really beneficial to them. I would recommend a positive story, however sometimes the opposite works wonders. Someone once came round to cheer me up in 2009 when I was not having the best of years for numerous reasons. This is roughly what he said, "I've got something that'll cheer you up: I saw a mate of mine down in Kent last week, he's going through a bit of a rough time and I said to him, you think you've got it bad, well I know this bloke who…" He stopped his story

and then just stared at me like he'd seen a ghost. I asked what was wrong, to which he replied, "Sorry mate, the story I told him was about you." I burst out laughing hysterically and then a few seconds later; so did he.

So he still managed to cheer me up, just not in the way he had planned. It seems on that particular day, when someone wanted to use the "you think you've got it bad" line; I was at the end of the line and no one had it worse. I'm not conceited enough to believe no one had it worse than me, but this was how it sounded, and what made me laugh so much.

3. Do something for charity or volunteer to join some local social project: once again you will be doing something invaluable, and in most cases you'll meet some new people who could become good friends.

4. Go and help a friend/family member with a chore: If you have to tidy your own garage, you tend to find any excuse to put it off until tomorrow, and as we know "tomorrow never comes." However, if we go and assist someone else to tidy their garage, we usually have a laugh doing it, and feel really great when the task is completed; because this other person now feels good.

5. Tell someone how much you appreciate them. This could be your partner, a family member, or a friend. This is probably the best suggestion of the lot. We take people for granted and often assume "they know how I feel about

them". Yet, if this was true, why do we often have personal doubts about whether other people genuinely like us or not? Not only this, but when we lose someone we are close to, we think to ourselves "if only I'd had chance to say ... to them". So why wait, say it today.

Remember, you joined a Military "Service". This means you chose to put the wellbeing of others ahead of your own. You were prepared to make the ultimate sacrifice to keep the civvies back home safe. Since it is part of your natural inclination to serve others, you may as well continue with this admirable trait by channelling it into other avenues when you are demobbed.

Chapter 23

Forgiveness

True forgiveness seems to be one of the hardest things for us to do, yet it is preached in almost all religions. The trouble is, when you hold on to any resentment towards another human being, it is not them who suffers, but you. You are the one experiencing the negative emotions of anger, whilst they are usually going about their lives oblivious to the bitterness you are holding on to.

We can start the process of forgiveness by pardoning ourselves for past transgressions. Most of the time, we never intended to hurt other people by our actions, and if we have learnt by this mistake, we will not do it again. If you can view what you did in the past as a valuable lesson, rather than beating yourself up over it, you will be able to release any negative emotions of guilt, which will result in improved wellbeing.

Many of us who have served are naturally perfectionists and so feel the emotion of guilt much more than most other people when we fuck up. In any given moment, you are as perfect as you can be based on your intelligence and life experiences. Strive to improve yourself on a daily basis, and you cannot be asked to do more than that. Perfectionism is like trying to get to the edge of the Universe, just as you think you've got there, there is still a bit further to go; it's simply an impossible task.

I have noticed people in Civvy Street are often overly critical of simple mistakes made by co-workers, as if they never make an error themselves. Everyone errs from time to time, it's only human and it's how we learn to do things right next time. So if you ever feel the urge to join in with these kinds of people, take a pause, suspend judgment, and if possible, point out to these critics the error of their ways. They may slag you off behind your back, but this will be their problem, not yours. It has nothing to do with being "morally superior"; it's just better for your own personal wellbeing than to be one of the whingers, whiners, blamers and complainers.

Next, you can move on to forgive the people who have wronged you. Just like the ones who you may have hurt, these people may not be suffering any level of emotional distress over the event; only you again. If you've ever seen the TV show "My name is Earl", you will know he wrote out a long list of all the people he had ripped off in one way or another. The premise of the series was he had discovered the concept of "Karma" and then went about making things right for the people on his list. You could write a list of not just the people who you wronged, but also the people who mistreated you. Then simply write a letter to the two groups of people; apologies to your aggrieved, and forgiveness to your attackers. Not everyone will respond, or even care, but you will have done your bit and your conscience will have been wiped clean. You can move on with your life, and no longer waste any energy thinking about the past.

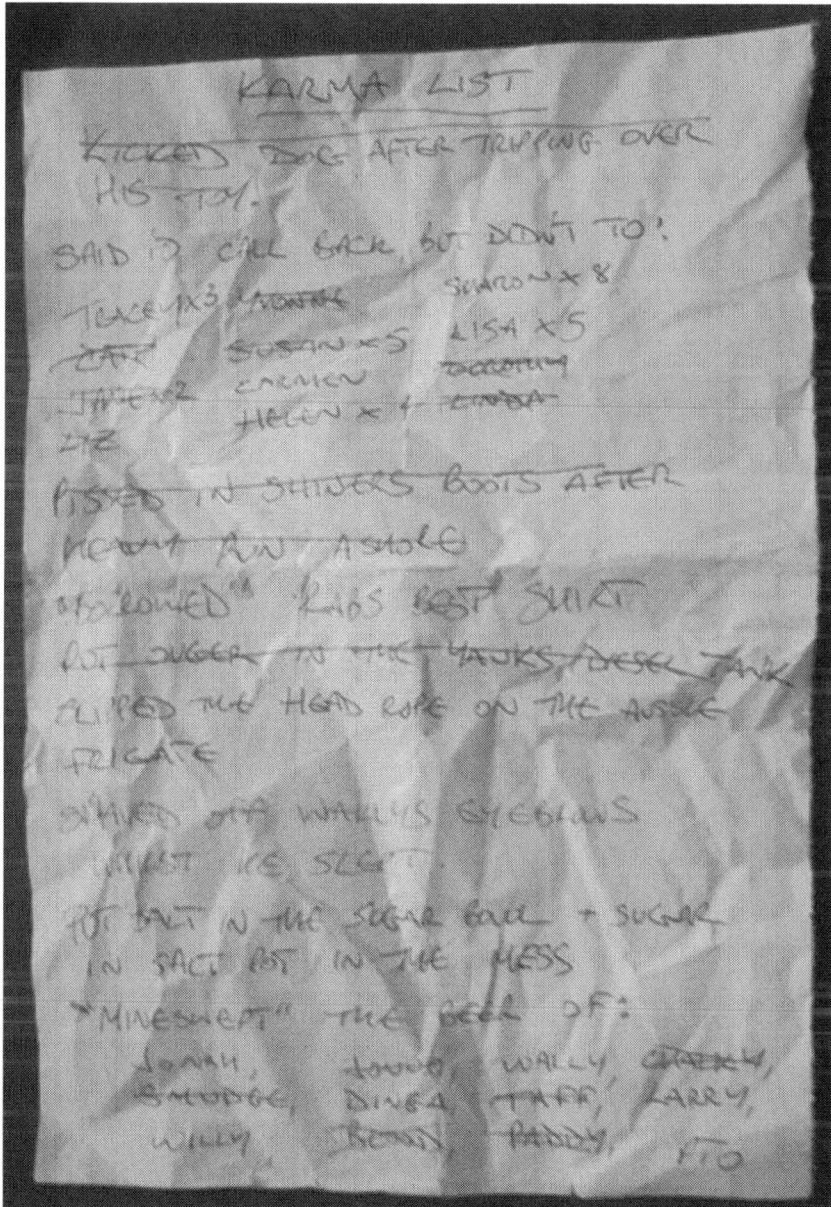

Image 25: Maybe a hard list to make amends for!

Chapter 24

The Law Of Attraction

Image 26: Now you know we're about to get "Deep"!

My first introduction to the subject of quantum mechanics came when a fellow therapist lent me a copy of the DVD, "What the bleep do we know". After watching it, I was hooked and have read quite a few books on the topic. During this time I also came across the movie "The Secret" by Rhonda Byrne and the book

"As a Man Thinketh" by James Allen. The underlining theme in much of these works is; we create our own reality with our thoughts. Although positive thinking wasn't a new concept to me, I never realised how deep you could go with its research.

The Law of Attraction as it is currently promoted suggests all we need to do is focus on the outcomes we desire, and the Universe will grant them. Unfortunately, this is a bit of an overgeneralised definition of how it actually works. I won't overload you with lots of heavy concepts today, if you want to learn more, there is plenty of material out there for you to conduct your own exploration.

I alluded slightly to this process in the introduction of this book when I mentioned "Branches of Psychology, Physics and Theology all say one thing of a similar nature; your beliefs create your reality." There are many passages in the Bible and other religious texts which confirm this, but many people overlook them, and only focus on the bits which justify their judgmental beliefs of superiority over others.

I'm oversimplifying here, but the "double slit" experiment used to define the Copenhagen Interpretation of Quantum Physics suggests; it is the observer who affects the outcomes of how events pan out. Meaning, if the observer expects one result, this is the one they will get. This is nothing, when you compare it to the latest thinking, which suggests we live in a "multiverse", and for every decision we make, another universe is created ad infinitum. The evidence put forward by John Gribbin in his fascinating book

"In search of the Multiverse" is really compelling, but a total head fuck!

"But how is this going to improve my wellbeing today?" you're probably thinking. Well, let's ignore the spiritual and theoretical physics aspects of the Law of Attraction, and just focus on the psychology for a moment. If you see the world as a scary, unfriendly and punishing environment, then you will only see the evidence to support this hypothesis. Yet the same is true when we think the opposite. If you see life as reasonably safe, full of friendly people and rewarding to those who take inspired action, guess what? You got it; you will see more and more evidence to back you up on this outlook. So the reality may be somewhere in the middle of these two conflicting ideologies, however why would you want to pick the negative one?

Karl Jung suggested "what we resist persists". In other words, if we keep our focus on the things we do not want in our lives, we will get more of them. The unconscious mind, as well as the Universe does not understand the word "don't". It just eliminates the word and focuses on the remainder of the statement, such as:

1. I don't want to be ill becomes "I want to be ill".
2. I don't want to think about the pain becomes "I want to think about the pain."
3. I don't want to be single and lonely becomes "I want to be single and lonely."

If any of this reflects your current condition, see if this is the way you have been communicating with yourself. Here's another example: Don't think of a fluffy pink rabbit with a drum.

Did you just get a brief flash of the image of a Duracell bunny? If not, I'll wager you thought of some sort of rabbit. So now you've seen it in action, it will be a good idea to look out for when you use this counterproductive term.

My personal explorations with the Law of Attraction have been quite productive both positively and negatively. I mentioned a few pages back that 2009 was not a particularly good year for me. Here's a quick list of some of the shite which occurred:

- Back and rib injury whilst pissed up on a bouncy castle in July!
- Hernia Operation on 7th December for injury received in May playing badminton, of all things!
- Given 2 months' notice on flat I rented above health centre on 9th December.
- Given 1 months' notice as a practitioner at health centre on 9th December.
- I had to have my cat put to sleep on 19th December, after a £2000 vet bill.

There were many more things which happened, but some I can't mention for legal reasons, which is a shame because I don't hold any resentment, whilst others aren't really of any interest to the point I want to make. Anyway, when I reflected on some of the things which had happened compared to my predominant thoughts, it became quite clear it was my own doing. One predominant thought was "I wish I had more time at home to study", and bam; my injuries gave me six months sat at home with nothing to do but read, or watch DVDs. The fact I lived above the health centre I was working at had caused a few tensions over the previous year, and so another predominant thought was "I need to move on from this place", and whoosh; the Universe gave me the push I had been reluctant to do for myself.

Obviously, one of my predominant thoughts was not "killing my cat"; taking him to the vet was one of the hardest things I've ever had to do. If I didn't have another cat and a dog to comfort me when I got back, I would have been writing some very dark poetry! I think this event was simply part of life's lessons.

Side note (Tangent): Since we're in the "airy fairy" section of the book, it's interesting to note it was 7 years since my last really crap year. Some say we go through 7 years cycles and if we do not learn the lesson, we repeat the cycle. Hmmm, best hope I've learnt the lesson this time!

I'll now share one of my positive experiences of the Law of Attraction, because we don't want to end this chapter on a downer do we:

In 2007 I had offered to perform a magic/mentalism act for the Yuletide party of a private group I knew some members of. My closing piece in the act had the potential to be lethal if I made the wrong choice from multiple options. For my patter, I wanted to bring the "Many Worlds Interpretation of Quantum Physics" into play. I had spent all day researching the theory and its proposer, Hugh Everett III. The trouble was; I couldn't find anything useable because it all went deep into the mathematical equations, and unless you were a physics professor, it wouldn't make much sense.

So at 2055hrs, with my head pounding I decided to have something to eat and just chill out in front of the TV for a bit. As previously mentioned, I didn't watch much telly. As I sat in front of the box with my snack, a show had just begun. It was a documentary following the son of Hugh Everett as he visited many people who knew him and his theory; so he could better understand both. Bingo, here was the information I had been looking for!

It would seem gleaning information with cooperation of the Universe is easier than materialising an Aston Martin DBS when you first start using the Law of Attraction consciously. However, as you begin to notice these little things turning up almost by coincidence, it will reinforce your belief in your own abilities to manifest, and who knows; a DBS may be just around the corner; I hope so anyway!

To assist in becoming a conscious creator of the life you desire, I suggest getting yourself a "Law of Attraction" diary or log, and every day fill in all the events you notice you have attracted to yourself through your thoughts. Write down both negative and positive occurrences. At first you may think it is just a coincidence, but I like Jung, do not believe in just coincidences; there is much evidence to support synchronicities. Over time, by keeping track like this, you will begin to control the way you think, and the scales will tip in favour of more beneficial things turning up in your life.

Keep your observations and desires to yourself, because apparently when you share, it will diminish your chances of these things turning up. This is why I only shared one of my lesser – albeit still important – manifestations, rather than one of the really big ones!

Here is a simplified version of how to get the Law of Attraction to work beneficially for you:

1. Focus your thoughts on what you desire, rather than on what you don't want.
2. The Universe works in mysterious ways, so the route to what you wish for may go on a winding path to get there. So allow it to do its thing, and avoid wasting your thoughts on how things are going to show up; simply believe they will turn up all in good time.
3. Of course, you will still need to do something to facilitate the process. When an opportunity presents itself, don't just sit on your arse contemplating whether this is it or

not. If you don't seize the moment, your rewards will usually be given on to someone who will.

4. Avoid gaining at the expense of others. There is plenty to go around, so don't begrudge other people for having more than you.

5. Be grateful for everything which shows up in your life, and take nothing for granted. Even when what appears to be crap shows up, still show appreciation. Difficult, I know, but for example; the end of one relationship could pave the way for the love of your life to show up.

6. Be patient! As soon as you have doubt, you have changed your thinking pattern back into a negative style and this will prevent things turning up.

7. If you cock up, you can always have another go, because in the Universe "Time is an illusion"; at least according to Einstein, and he was one smart dude.

As I said, there is so much information out there on this principle, you will easily find more than enough to keep you going if you want to delve even deeper.

Chapter 25

Surround Yourself With Life

Image 27: Who's afraid of the big bad wolf?!

It goes without saying; time spent with good friends is highly enjoyable and improves your mood tremendously. Sometimes the same can be said about time with family members! Be certain to get out and about to see your friends at least once a week, more if possible. Not just for a "dripping session", but arrange to go out and do something.

Even, if like me, you enjoy time in solitude, it is important to still surround yourself with life. This could be as simple as getting some house plants to brighten your living room up. I know it sounds weird, but it really does affect the energy in a room. For example, if you go into a church on an average day when there are no flowers on display, it feels totally different to going into one after a wedding when it is full of them, doesn't it?

The first plants I got after getting divorced were cacti, because they are easy to look after. Eleven years on and they are still going strong, and have survived several moves of home. One even flowers every couple of years and really brightens the place up. I have many other houseplants now, and so looking after their specific needs takes up more time than the cacti, but not too much more.

The greatest mood enhancing thing to acquire - in my opinion - is a pet. It has been shown in studies, stroking a pet reduces stress quite significantly. In fact, the idea of pets helping sufferers of PTSD has been so successful in the United States, there is a great charitable organisation called "Pets for Vets" who rehome abandoned animals with injured service personnel. Maybe someone could set up something similar in the UK to take the strain off the RSPCA?

With so many animals being destroyed each year unnecessarily, why not visit your local animal shelter, and give a second chance to one of the poor unfortunate critters looking for someone to love them. It breaks my heart to see an animal being mistreated or cast aside because the novelty factor has worn off. An animal is a living being with its own personality, as you will find out if you get one.

As you may be able to tell, I am a bit of a soft touch when it comes to animals. I got my first cat, Darth, from the "Cats

Protection League", and a year later he brought an abandoned stray home with him. I kept giving it a little bit of food, but it got no bigger, and so I took it to the vet; had it de-flead, wormed, and neutered. I asked around the neighbourhood if anyone owned him, and then when he had healed from his surgery; I opened the door and gave him the option to leave. He chose to stay, and as you can see by the picture, Dooku is fit and healthy, some eight years later. And yes, I'm that nerdy to name my cats after Star Wars characters!

Even my dog had a sorry time to begin with. I got him when he was eight months old, and was his third owner. The first were an old couple who clearly didn't understand what a handful a Siberian husky pup can be. The second was a lad in the RAF, who had just been put on forty-eight hour standby for the Gulf. Because he had just split from his girlfriend, he had no one to take care of the dog if he was deployed. My girlfriend at the time was looking for a horse, spotted the ad for him, and so I ended up with a dog! He was very hard work for the first couple of years, but well worth the effort in the long run. A dog as they say is "man's best friend" and as well as being great loyal companions, you are forced to get off your arse and exercise them every day without fail; so two benefits for the price of one. Cats are great if you don't want to be tied down like you are with a dog. If you have a cat flap, providing there is food and water available, the cat will come and go as it pleases. Yet despite their outwardly nonchalant attitude, they always seem to know when to appear to cheer you up.

If you don't have the time for a larger animal, then even something like a domestic rat can provide hours of entertainment, and are reasonably low maintenance.

Maybe you are allergic to fur, so why not get a fish tank. There is definitely something therapeutic about sitting watching fish swimming about; this is why they are often found in Doctors and Dentists waiting rooms. If this sounds too much like hard work, you could simply get a single goldfish!

If the idea of maintaining plants or animals doesn't appeal to you right now, then there is always the option of going for a walk in nature. Get out into somewhere green and just watch life going about its business, totally oblivious to the trials and tribulations of human beings. This leads me nicely on to my final tip, so if you haven't got one already; now is the time to get your pen or pencil ready for the question I'm going to ask you at the end of it.

Chapter 26

Connect With Your Higher Self

Image 28: So Deep; you'll need a SSBN to get back!

Religion is a sensitive subject and one best avoided in polite conversation. I personally think it is a totally personal choice and should be left to the individual to find his/her own correct path. So I want to assure you with this final tip I am not promoting, slandering or trying to convert anyone to any particular religion or spiritual discipline. Whether you are religious, spiritual, or an atheist, I would like you to simply suspend judgment and look at what follows objectively. If you think it's all a load of bollocks - or worse - at the end of the tip; this is fine. You are entitled to have your opinion; but so am I, and so is every other person on the planet too.

We can all agree; there is much going on in the Universe which we cannot currently understand or explain. We can also agree there is some sort of creative force or energy in the Universe, yes? If there wasn't, plants, animals, and of course human beings wouldn't exist and grow. What you call this energy is irrelevant. You can call it God, Allah, The Great Mystery, Magic, the electro-magnetic field of quantum physics, or whatever you like. These are just different words created by man to describe something intangible. For the sake of this tip, let's agree to disagree on what to call it, and just accept it exists; and this is all we need to know. We may dislike change, but in reality nothing is the same from one moment to the next; change is a constant. So connecting with this unseen force will put you in alignment with what is happening at all times everywhere.

No person, no religion, and no dogma can tell you exactly how to connect with your higher self, or whatever you wish to call it. They may provide guidance on possible routes, they may tell you how you should live your life, they may tell you how you will connect when you are dead, but not how to experience this connection whilst you are still alive. No one can experience it for you, so how could they tell you? Personal experience is just that; personal, and there is no right or wrong way to do it. Providing it doesn't interfere with anyone else, you will be fine.

Our conscious mind likes to see us as separate entities, yet at the quantum level there really is no separation between you, me, every living thing on the planet; in fact everything in the entire Universe. Even the word itself says this if you look at it: The prefix "Uni" meaning one or singular, and "verse" makes you think of a poem or a song doesn't it? So there you have it, "One Song".

Side Note (Tangent): This may sound kind of weird - or even weirder after the preceding tips - but as I often do when I'm walking my dog; I contemplate the meaning in, and of things and words. One day I was thinking about the Universe and came to the realisation I have just mentioned. Then the next day I was listening to a Dr Wayne Dyer audio program I had just purchased, and he said exactly the same thing. Freaky or what?!

One of the best descriptions I've found for what is going on in the Universe; doesn't come from a science book, nor from religious texts, but is in fact from an alien race in the Sci-Fi series "Babylon 5":

"We believe that the Universe itself is conscious in a way we can never truly understand. It is engaged in a search for meaning, so

it breaks itself apart; investing its own consciousness in every form of life. We are the Universe trying to understand itself."

If this sounds a bit too deep for you right now, simply consider how if nothing else we are connected by the ground we walk on and the air we breathe.

To conclude this series of bonus tips, I will offer a few suggestions of finding a way to connect with something more than just your average everyday experience:

1. Get into Nature: At the end of the last tip, I suggested going out into nature and just observing. The realisation of humans not being quite as important in the grand scheme of the Universe as we think we are can suddenly dawn on you when you see bumble bees busying about, totally oblivious to your existence. You can then perhaps appreciate what a fantastic gift life and the planet we share truly are, and maybe, just maybe decide to respect both a little more. Simply find a quiet spot if you can on a nice day, and just sit and watch. Let go of any negative thoughts, and after a few minutes you will feel something. What this feeling is, you will need to discover for yourself. So don't delay, do it today!

2. Yoga: although my only personal experience of this has been using the Wii Fit, it is something I plan on giving a proper go one day. As well as being good for the mind,

and spirit; it is also good for physical health. Tai Chi and Qi Gong also provides similar benefits, but as yet I haven't tried them, so can't really comment. However, if you watch people doing it, they certainly seem quite chilled out.

3. Meditation: This is probably the best way of experiencing your connection with "all that is". I'm no expert at it, and don't do it as often as I could, yet find it a very refreshing experience when I do dedicate the time. There are numerous methods for doing meditation. One method is to repeat the sound "ohm" as you breathe out. You don't even need to say it out loud if you're worried the neighbours may think you've gone all bohemian!

Here's a quick meditation I use, to get you started: find somewhere to sit comfortably and place your hands on your lap. Close your eyes and begin to focus on your breathing. Breathe in through your nose, filling your diaphragm, and out through your mouth slowly. As you feel your body starting to relax, picture a bright red love heart and keep your focus on this one image. Once you can keep this picture in mind, add the sound of the word "love" to your focus. Once you have this mastered, you can try to alternate between breathing in "love", and breathing away "tension". For this image, picture blowing away a dark cloud. In the beginning your mind will keep racing, and other thoughts will enter your mind. This is normal, you just need to be persistent and overtime these kinds of thoughts will get less and less. To start off with just try it for 5 minutes and see how you feel, and then progressively spend more and more time in meditation until you find a good routine which works for you.

4. Finally, my very last tip is to explore religions and spiritual paths other than your own. This won't make you a blasphemer, and you do not have to convert either; unless you should choose to. If merely reading the teachings of a faith were enough to cause your eternal damnation, then most Religious and Spiritual Leaders would be truly fucked!

    We spend way too much time arguing over who is right or wrong, the differences between interpretations of ancient texts, and the name - or names - for whatever is in charge of the Universe. Each camp believes they have exclusivity on being right, yet many of their followers do not even know the history of where their beliefs originated, or when they were actually written down. I have spent many years reading books on most of the world's religions and can assure you, the commonalities tend to be the most important passages in all of these works. If we see most other people on the planet want the same things we do, we may be able to judge them less and prevent future wars. When this day eventually arrives, books like the one you have just read will no longer need to be written. This is a day I'm certainly looking forward to.

I'd like to end with a quote from "The Princess of Babylon" by Voltaire:

"Everyone acknowledged: that the gods had instituted Kings for no other cause than every day to give festivals; upon condition that they should be diversified. For life is too short to be made any other use of. For law suits, intrigues, wars, the altercations of theologians which consume human life; are horrible & absurd. That man is born only for happiness, that he would not passionately & incessantly pursue pleasure were he not designed for it. That the essence of human nature is to enjoy oneself, and all the rest is folly."

Before our time together ends for now, here is the question I have been referring to: Did you spot the undercurrent, or sort of hidden lesson contained in these 10 tips?

Write your answer in the space below, before turning the page:

Look out for the full version of my 10 Tips Book to see if your answer is the same as mine!

If you found the contents of either the videos or this book (hopefully both) to be beneficial to you, I would love to hear your success story. I can't promise to respond to every one I receive, but I'll do my best.

Please feel free to email me at stuart@skilledexforces.com

Fare Well & I Salute You.

Stuart

About The Author

Stuart Welbourn left school with only minimal qualifications. This was part due to a poor attendance record, part due to being in the guinea pig year for GCSE's, but mainly due to a long ambition to join the Royal Navy like his Grandfather before him. In March 1989 this ambition was realised, and after completing his training as a Sonar Operator, he joined HMS Sheffield and served on her during the first Gulf War. From 1992 he spent the rest of his naval career at HMS St. Vincent in London from where he was medically discharged in November 1996. For his resettlement he studied and qualified in Hypnotherapy and Psychotherapy, with part of his training being completed in Harley Street, London.

As a newly married and freshly trained Psychotherapist, he ran his own local practice for a couple of years; gaining extra Diplomas in Dream Analysis and Neuro-Linguistic Programming during this time. Stuart then moved to a newly opened Health Centre in 1999 and worked there for 11 years. During this time he consumed tome after tome, attended numerous workshops, courses and seminars on subjects as diverse as Past Life Regression, Memory Techniques, and Relationship Counselling. Stuart also gained diplomas in Complete Mind Therapy, E.F.T. and two Theologies based subjects. He has been a member of both the "Hypnotherapy Practitioners Guild" and the "Hypnotherapy Practitioners Association".

Stuart has regularly appeared on local BBC radio sharing insights on a variety of subjects, and has also provided Therapeutic Services for a popular day time TV show.

Stuart gave up one-to-one treatments at the end of 2009 to concentrate on providing help to a wider audience; in particular, Service Personnel, and he is the mastermind behind two websites dedicated to this task. At the time of this book going to print, both these websites are under construction. The first of these will be an International Directory of Veteran Owned Businesses, SkilledExForces.Com. The second, SucceedAfterService.Com aims to help with Military Transition; primarily in the field of self-employment. It will provide the tools, information and resources needed for success in Civvy Street. One of these is the "Interrogation of the Experts" audio series, where Stuart has interviewed some of the biggest names in their chosen fields to provide invaluable advice for the budding military entrepreneur.

Stuart is a self-confessed "studyaholic" and this habit is satisfied with learning as much as possible about the "Mind", the "Universe", and our connection with them. Since 2008, he has devoted the greatest proportion of his study time to learning about business success; marketing in particular.

When he takes time for himself, Stuart enjoys walks in the countryside with his Siberian husky, riding motorbikes and the occasional pint of premium Lager!

Chapter 27

I Couldn't Be That Cruel!

I have many books in my personal library where a question has been posed just like the one I did at what you thought was the end of the book. Well, as an Ex-Matelot I first have to say "weeeee, you bit!" Secondly, as an Ex-Serviceman, I also know this will be the page most likely to be torn out of the book should you leave it loafing!

But fortunately, I'm also a Psychotherapist and I'm not going to leave you wondering what the answer to the question is, at least as far as I'm concerned. Your opinions will be just as valid as mine, but since I'm writing it; it is only fair if I share what I had in mind.

Being Present Minded

In virtually all, if not all of the bonus tips, there was one thing you had to be doing with your thoughts. This was to be conscious in the moment, or present minded as some refer to it. When we are concentrating on what is happening to us right now, we cannot be thinking about what has happened to us in the past, nor can we worry about what the future may or may not hold.

Here comes the weird and wonderful "thought exercise" I alluded to earlier in the book. I used to share it with some of my clients to demonstrate the truth of this statement: "Unless we are in physical pain, every second of our lives is, in reality; peaceful and calm":

"If I were to pull out a gun and point it at you, in this very moment everything is actually peaceful. Nothing is happening to you physically, it's only in your mind. You are afraid that I may pull the trigger and you would be dead, but this is putting your thoughts in the future, and only one possible future. I could pull the trigger and a little flag could pop out of the end with the word "BANG!" on it. It could be unloaded, it could be a water pistol, or I could simply put it away. So until, I actually pull the trigger, you do not know, and you are actually fine in the present moment. Then if I were to fire a loaded gun, your moments of "now" would be over and everything would still be calm and peaceful!"

PTSD may make it difficult to maintain a focus on the present for long, especially when unexpected events set off a flashback. However, if you keep using some of the 10 bonus tips regularly; you may find your symptoms plague you a little less often, the more you do them. As I said at the start of the bonus tips section, they are really just an outline for another book I may write at some point, and I am sharing them with you to improve your wellbeing, and not to remove any PTSD symptoms directly.

Oh, there's just one more thing, I'm not sure if I've already mentioned this in my book or not. So just to cover my ass, I need to say:

If you believe you have any physical or mental ailments of any kind; Always consult a Doctor!!

This really does conclude my book; I hope it serves you nearly as well as you have served your country.

Always implement what you learn as soon as humanly possible. You have my sincerest hopes for success in your endeavours.

Stuart

"Fide Tibi Et Semper Pete Veritatem"

(Believe In Thyself and Always Seek the Truth)

Notes

Notes

Printed in Great Britain
by Amazon

35977562R00108